Fears, Stress and Trauma: Helping Children Cope

Part I: Overview of Fears and Stress
Part II: Coping with Trauma
Part III: Facilitator's Guide

Edward H. Robinson, Joseph C. Rotter
Sandra L. Robinson, Mary Ann Fey
Joanne E. Vogel

Fears, Stress, and Trauma
Helping Children Cope.

Based on a publication developed by the Department of Educational Psychology at the University of South Carolina in Columbia and originally published through a grant from the Overseas School Advisory Council awarded to the Association of International Schools in Africa.

ISBN 1-56109-100-6

CAPS Press
A Division of Counseling Outfitters, L.L.C.
PO Box 35077
Greensboro, NC 27425-5077

This publication was funded in part by the U.S. Department of Education, Office of Educational Research and Improvement, Contract No. ED-99-CO-0014. Opinions expressed in this publication do not necessarily reflect the positions of the U.S. Department of Education, OERI, or ERIC/CASS.

CAPS PRESS

Contents

Part I: Overview of Fears and Stress

Section 1: Overview of Fears and Stress in Children

Section 2: Fear-Specific Activities

Section 3: Fear-Prevention Activities

Section 4: Appendices

Part II: Coping with Trauma

Section 1: Helping Children in a Time of Crisis

Section 2: Trauma-Specific Activities

Section 3: Stress-Reducing Activities

Section 4: Appendices

Part III: Facilitator's Guide

Introduction

Session 1: Orientation

Session 2: Primary Prevention

Session 3: School and Classroom Activities

Session 4: Helping High-Risk or Children

Session 5: Helping Children During a Crisis

Session 6: Helping Children Who Are Not Coping Well

Session 7: Stress/Fear and the Family

Session 8: Developing an Action Plan

List of Handouts

Part I

Part III

Preface

There are a number of things that excite me about *Fears, Stress and Trauma: Helping Children Cope*. First, it clearly responds to a present and growing need for a resource book that will help counselors, teachers and educators to better understand how fears, phobias, anxiety and stress develop in children (K-8), and how they (children) can be assisted in successfully coping with omnipresent fears and stress. Second, in a highly gratifying and much needed departure from the usual practice of offering up generalized "cookbook" approaches, the authors have developed 76 specific activities. Each of the activities is designed to assist a child in coping with a particular aspect of fear or stress. Some are designed to assist children in coping with extant fears and stress, while others focus on fear prevention, stress reduction or helping high-risk students. A third attractive and most useful feature of this book is a facilitator's guide, which will assist the counselor, teacher or educator to more effectively intervene with children and to make better use of the activities provided. Fourth, this is not a book filled with pipe dreams. The authors have validated the concepts and activities through extensive field testing with schools and students in this country and overseas.

My list of what I like about *Fears, Stress and Trauma: Helping Children Cope* could go on endlessly. Suffice to say it is a book that is both practical and substantive and will be of inestimable use to counselors, teachers and educators.

Garry R. Walz
Director, ERIC/CASS

About the Authors

Edward H. Robinson, III, Ph.D., is a professor in the Department of Child, Family and Community Sciences at the University of Central Florida in Orlando, Florida.

Joseph C. Rotter, Ph.D., is a professor in the Department of Educational Psychology at the University of South Carolina in Columbia, South Carolina.

Sandra L. Robinson, Ph.D., is Dean of the College of Education at the University of Central Florida in Orlando, Florida.

Mary Ann Fey, M.Ed., NCC, is an elementary school counselor at St. Joseph's Elementary School in Columbia, South Carolina.

Joanne E. Vogel, Ph.D., is a clinical associate professor in the Department of Child, Family and Community Services at the University of Central Florida in Orlando, Florida, and a mental health counselor in private practice.

Acknowledgements

The authors would like to thank the following individuals for contributing their creative talents in formulating some of the activities included in this book:

Liz Azukas
Rita Weil Caldwell
Janine Collins
Andrea Hammond
Holly Harris
Chris Karper
Amy Longstreth
Ursula Patterson
Gregory R. Price
Donna Rooney
Kathryn Tagye
Rachel Taub
Jackie Reilly

How to Use This Book

Fears, Stress, and Trauma: Helping Children Cope is meant for teachers, school counselors, school psychologists and school administrators.

Part I: Overview of Fears and Stress

Part I: Overview of Fears and Stress contains activities to complement the various curricular areas of a typical elementary and middle school. These activities are designed to integrate into normal instruction without the disruption that a separate "Unit" on fears or stress would entail. To make the activities easier to use, each one includes the curricular areas into which it would fit (i.e., Language Arts, Social Studies, etc.), the grade levels and group size for which it is suitable, and the approximate time necessary for completion. **Part I** is divided into the following sections:

> **Section 1** is an introduction to the origin of fears and stress in children and to the theory that underlies the authors' model for successful coping.

> **Section 2** deals with fear-specific activities; that is, activities contributing to the alleviation of the effects of fear and to specific fears such as fear of the dark, monsters, insects, etc.

> **Section 3** comprises general activities used for the prevention of fear and to bolster children's feelings of security, self-worth, and control.

> **Section 4** includes four appendices: **Appendix I-A** presents a model of counseling which can be used with children who have suffered a trauma or who have not developed successful coping skills. **Appendix I-B** includes a quick reference guide to common disorders associated with fears and stress that may necessitate outside referrals to other professionals or specialists. **Appendix I-C** is a bibliography of children's books, arranged by fear, author and grade level, which teachers or counselors can use for bibliotherapeutic purposes. **Appendix I-D** is a list of other resources that may be helpful to the educator interested in developing a collection of materials dealing with fears and stress.

Part II: Coping with Trauma

Part II: Coping with Trauma contains information regarding what happens to children as a result of traumatic events and how to manage the after-effects of such situations. Pertinent models to use during crises such as Critical Incident Stress Debriefing (CISD) and adaptations of this model such as the Adapted Family Debriefing Model (AFDM) and Critical Incident Stress Management will be outlined. Both trauma-specific and stress-reducing activities are included to use as necessary after either an individual or collective crisis. **Part II** is divided into the following sections:

Section 1 defines a traumatic event and discusses common symptoms following exposure to such events. In addition, this section includes mediating factors and outlines models for handling such incidents.

Section 2 offers a number of trauma-specific activities to be used either individually or as a group intervention.

Section 3 includes stress-reducing activities to help alleviate the feelings of stress often associated with traumatic situations.

Section 4 includes five Appendices: **Appendix II-A** discusses high-risk children in schools. **Appendix II-B** is a quick guide of things to do before a crisis or traumatic event. **Appendix II-C** is a quick guide for parents about how to help children cope. **Appendix II-D** is a quick guide to the Adapted Family Debriefing Model (AFDM) used in coping with the aftermath of crises or traumatic events. **Appendix II-E** includes a listing of resources for trauma recovery.

Part III: Facilitator's Guide

Part III is divided into eight sessions. The purpose of this guide is to provide training to teachers and counselors who wish to learn how to help children cope with fears and stress.

Session 1 provides an opportunity for participants to share something briefly about themselves and establish an atmosphere of relaxed sharing as they begin to explore the typical fears and stress of children.

Session 2 addresses the three levels of primary prevention: developmental, high-risk and treatment. An overview of the levels is presented, followed by an in-depth study of the first level of prevention (developmental) and related intervention strategies.

Session 3 provides teachers and school counselors with ideas for activities they can do with children to help them develop the knowledge and skills necessary for coping with fears and stress.

Session 4 helps teachers and school counselors recognize potential high-risk children and develop the knowledge and skills necessary for helping these children.

Session 5 helps teachers and school counselors develop an understanding of how to help children cope with their fears and stress during either a collective or individual crisis.

Session 6 helps teachers and school counselors develop an understanding of how to help children who are not coping well in their lives because of the effect of fears and stress.

Session 7 focuses on fear and stress as family issues. Although isolated incidents may trigger fear and stress, their effect on children often results from the amount of advanced preparation parents have made and their ability to effectively follow up on stressful situations.

Session 8 emphasizes the three levels of prevention with a focus on infusion of activities on fear and stress into the daily curriculum. This final session is the most important part of the training, for it is through the plan of action developed by the teachers and counselors that the program will or will not reach success.

Part I

Overview of Fears and Stress

Section I
Overview of Fears and Stress in Children

Introduction

Childhood is generally a positive time of life filled with promise, hope and wonder. It can also be a time of stress and fear as the demands of a rapidly changing world and the rising expectations of modern life take their toll. Although learning to deal with stressors is a normal part of growing up, many children develop inadequate or inappropriate coping strategies. Researchers have linked this inability to cope appropriately to the increasing rate of teen (Spirito, Francis, Overholser, & Frank, 1996) and pre-teen suicide (Swanston, Nunn, Oates, Tebbutt, & O'Toole, 1999), substance abuse (Greydanus, 1991), teen pregnancy (Burnett, 2002; Franklin & Corcoran, 2000) and academic failure (Greydanus, 1991; Wood, 2001). Since the consequences of fear and stress can be so serious, it behooves us to be cognizant of the signs of fear and stress among children and to be aware of activities and strategies that may help to alleviate or prevent their deleterious effects.

The purpose of this publication, then, is to offer to teachers, counselors, school psychologists and other professionals working with children a brief introduction to the topic of children's fears and stress and a guide to activities and strategies that can be integrated into the curriculum from kindergarten though eighth grade. These activities are meant to be useful for purposes of prevention and, in some cases, remediation of the effects of fears and stress. In addition, they are structured so as to fit within the typical elementary school or middle school curriculum rather than treated as one more "subject" added to an already over-crowded school day.

As part of the introduction to the guide, definitions of the various types of fears will be presented and the results of recent investigations into the nature of fears in children will be discussed.

Fears, Phobias, Anxiety and Stress

Fear can be defined as an affective (feeling), cognitive (thinking), motoric (behaving) and physiological (bodily changing) response to a perceived threat. Generally, it is a response to a specific object or concept, such as a snake or being left alone. Fear is a normal part of the growth and development process and can be an important tool for self-preservation. Faced with a fear object, such as an oncoming truck, a child's fear response (distress, recognition of real danger, increased heart rate and adrenaline, and fleeing) is quite appropriate and even necessary for the continued existence of the organism. As the pioneer in the study of fears, G. Stanley Hall stated, "The pedagogic problem is not to eliminate fear, but to gauge it to the power of proper reactions" (1897, p. 242).

Phobias are a type of fear which is largely irrational and out of proportion to the threat. The focus of a phobia is usually specific, such as the fear of flying or of heights, yet the source is not necessarily immediately threatening to the victim. Phobias in children are often associated with school.

Anxiety is a feeling of uneasiness or doom whose source is uncertain and vague. The person suffering from anxiety may not be able to pinpoint the cause nor even specify the nature of the doom that the anxiety portends. Nevertheless, the effects of anxiety can be as debilitating as if the source were real and specific. For an in-depth discussion of etiological considerations and specific issues dealing with diagnosis and classification of anxiety-related disorders, the reader may wish to consult the *International Handbook of Phobic and Anxiety Disorders in Children and Adolescents,* edited by Ollendick, King and Yule (1994); *Anxiety and Phobic Disorders: A Pragmatic Approach,* by Silverman and Kurtines (1996); the *Diagnostic and Statistical Manual of Mental Disorders 4th edition, Text Revision* (2000), or Appendix I-B included in Section 4 at the end of Part 1.

Stress can be defined as tension caused by a positive or negative event. It can serve as a warning signal or can lead to problems such as tension headaches, ulcers and other physiological and psychological impairments. "Stress isn't just a catchall complaint; it's being linked to heart disease, immune deficiency and memory loss…The worst part, is we inflict it on ourselves" (Adler, 1999). Recent investigations at the University of South Florida School of Medicine have linked stress with the loss of short-term and intermediate memory (T. Freeman, personal communication, September 3, 2000). Deadlines and overwork, lack of sleep, rapid changes, familial and environmental crises, and culture shock are examples of sources of stress in both children and adults.

The fear cycle in children is illustrated in the following figure:

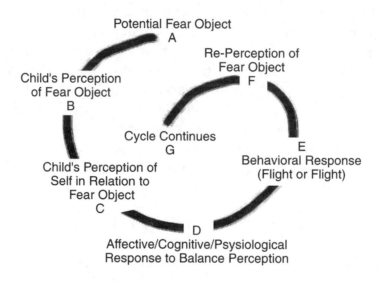

Figure I.I
Conceptualization of the Fear Cycle

Learning to cope with fears is a part of the normal process of child development. It is when children develop inappropriate responses or inadequate coping strategies that fears become a problem. Studies have shown that one in five children suffers from debilitating forms of test anxiety that inhibit school performance (Deffenbacher, Michaels, Michaels, & Daley, 1986; Deffenbacher & Michaels, 1981; King, Mietz, Tinney, & Ollendick, 1995; Phillips, 1978). King, Mietz, Tinney and Ollendick (1995) state, "…it seems difficult to refute the observation that severe evaluation anxiety in youngsters is frequently associated with marked psychopathology and diagnostic heterogeneity" (p. 53). Craske (1997) outlines the issue of comorbidity indicating that almost forty percent of children with anxiety disorders may have accompanying disorders. One in ten children will develop

...ral and academic deficie...ies...................in...en children's fears cited by one group of teachers include.......................obinson, Robinson, & Whetsell, 1988):

Teachers' Perceptions of Typical Fears in Children

1. Change of school	6. Death	11. Ghosts
2. Failure at school	7. Darkness	12. Loss
3. Being alone	8. Homework	13. Not being accepted
4. Family strife	9. Strangers	14. Nuclear War
5. Punishment	10. Monsters	15. Thieves

An international study of children's fears (Robinson, et al.) surveyed the fears of children between the ages of four and fourteen and included subjects from the United States, South America, Africa and the Middle East. Through the use of a structured interview, the children cited most often the following fear objects:

Children's Overall Perceptions of Fears in Six Countries

1. Darkness	6. Monsters
2. Ghosts	7. Other people in general
3. Isolation	8. Specific people (robbers, etc.)
4. Nightmares	9. Being lost
5. Punishment	10. Teachers

However, children from different cultures do not necessarily fear the same objects nor do they cite them in the same order. Different environments can contribute to different perceptions of what should and should not be frightening. For example, city children who are not exposed to natural phenomena would be less likely to cite particular animals as being fear provoking than would rural children. Conversely, traffic would not be a great source of fear in rural settings. A comparison of the top ten fears of children from the U.S.A., Ecuador, Liberia, Australia and China demonstrates this difference rather clearly.

... understand...

understand any differenc...
cognitive functioning (Plonk, 1999, ..., 1997).
From the lists above, it is obvious that there are some e..vir.................ence, that can be ascribed to the specific circumstances of a given client's environment. For instance, one eight-year-old from Nigeria indicates his top two fears as the ghosts of his ancestors and the harmiton (a hot, dry wind off the Sahara Desert). The first is consistent with the belief system of his culture and the second with his geographic location. Another consideration discussed extensively in the literature is that of gender differences. Numerous studies report that females are more fearful than males and that there are some differences in fear objects (Craske, 1997). Svensson and Oest (2000) found no significant difference in levels of fears between females and males in a recent study of Swedish children introducing the notion that culture may be a mitigating variable in sex differences. Others argue that such differences are more a matter of methodology issues in measurement. Still others contend that cognitive functioning makes a difference. Plonk (1999) found that there were no discernable differences between the fears of gifted children and normal children. Ramirez and Kratochwill (1997) found little evidence of differences between the fears of children with and without mental retardation but found a slight difference in the level of fears. They concluded that "...there are more similarities than differences between these two groups in their most prevalent fears. What is evident is that developmental differences seem to be consistent."

Fear objects apparently change with age and maturation (Muris & Merckelbach, 2000). The fear of large animals is common in younger school-age children but diminishes in older elementary-age children. Fear of death is not prevalent in the early years but begins to be a concern for children in the elementary grades. Imaginary fear objects such as monsters, ghosts and witches diminish in middle school-age children and are replaced with, among other things, fears of nuclear war, muggers and failure in school. The fears of adolescence seem to revolve around personal and sexual identity, social acceptance, purpose in life and failure. Beginning in middle school and increasing through the high school years, representation of fear objects tends to become vague. Thus, anxiety, rather than fear, may be a more useful term for a young person's reaction in the later school years (Rotter & Robinson, 1987).

Primary Prevention Model

The information contained in this introduction is designed to aid parents, counselors, and teachers in understanding the many facets of fear including those fears encountered through the course of normal development and those fears occurring in response to traumatic situations. When implementing a program to address children's fears, it is beneficial to consider three levels of primary prevention as a guiding model (See Figure I-2). These three levels include a focus on children's developmental fears, a focus on children with increased or high risk of developing fearful responses, and a focus on those children who exhibit significant disturbances in behavior that warrant treatment. Regardless of the level where the counselor, parent, or teacher chooses to intervene, the concepts of control, security, and self-worth should be an integral part of the process while also addressing the identified fear object. These concepts are discussed in more detail below as part of the section entitled "The Foundations for Successful Coping

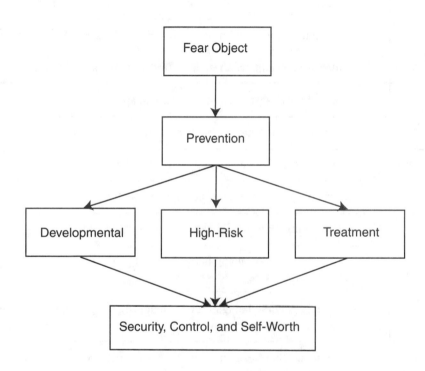

Figure 1.2
Primary Prevention of Children's Fears

Knowing some of the common developmental fears will help parents, teachers, and counselors in identifying potential fear objects or experiences. Table 1.3 summarizes normative data on the chronological appearance of children's fears taken from a number of studies.

Table 1.3
Normative Data on Children's Fears

Age	Fears
0-6 months	Loss of support, loud noises, sudden movement
7-12 months	Strangers, sudden appearance of large objects, loud noises
1 year	Separation from parent, strangers, injury, toilet
2 years	Large animals, dark rooms, large objects and machines, loud noises, sudden changes in personal environment
3 years	Dark rooms, masks, large animals, snakes, separation from parent
4 years	Dark rooms, noise at night, large animals, snakes, separation from parent
5 years	Wild animals, bodily injury, dark, bad people, separation from parent
6 years	Ghosts, monsters, witches, dark, storms, being alone, thunder and lightning
7 years	Dark, monsters, storms, being lost, kidnapping, being alone, scary dreams
8 years	Dark, people (kidnapper, robber, mugger), guns/weapons, being alone, animals
9 years	Dark, lost, bad dreams, bodily harm/accident, being alone
10 years	Dark, people, bad dreams, punishment, strangers
11 years	Dark, being alone, bad dreams, being hurt by someone, being sick, tests, grades
12 years	Dark, punishment (being in trouble, bad grades), being alone, being hurt or taken away, tests, grades
13 years	Crime in general, being hurt or kidnapped, being alone, war in general and nuclear war, bad grades, tests, punishment
14 years+	Failure at school, personal relations, war, tests, sex issues (pregnancy, AIDS), being alone, family concerns

Source: Craske, 1997; Croak & Knox, 1971; Jersild & Holmes, 1935; Kellerman, 1981; Maurer, 1965; Morris & Kratochwill, 1983; Muris & Merckelbach, 2000; Svensson & Oest, 1999; Robinson, Robinson, & Whetsell, 1988.

The goal of developmental interventions, as part of the primary prevention model, is to assist all children in developing the best skills possible for successfully meeting the demands of life in the present and in the future. To do this, counselors might want to send newsletters or hold parenting workshops to educate parents about developmental fears in addition to the dos and don'ts of parenting with regard to children's fears. Examples of the dos would include the following: Do encourage children to communicate, do listen to children, and do help them explore strategies to defeat the monsters in their lives. However, don't use fear to secure discipline, don't make fun of children's fears, and don't dismiss children's fears as fanciful or imaginary. This level of prevention should focus on helping children to develop a sense of their strengths while finding opportunities for children to engage in success experiences. A focus on increasing effective interpersonal skills would be appropriate as part of developmental prevention strategies.

The second level of primary prevention, high-risk children, includes those children who have experienced collective or personal disasters in their lives. Collective disasters might include earthquakes, tornadoes, hurricanes, fire, war, and terrorist acts. Personal disasters include such things as the loss of a parent through death or divorce, bodily injury, frequent moves, changing schools, school failure, and family strife. Any incident that increases the stress level of children places that child at risk for developing fear-related impairments or disorders. At the same time, many children can experience such incidents and cope successfully, especially when children learn how to release the tension brought on by crisis situations. For this level of prevention, the counselor will want to deal first with the specific issue affecting the child or children then help to re-establish a sense of control, self-worth, and security.

The third level of prevention is helping the child who is already experiencing fear-related problems. The longer fear-related problems persist the more difficult it is to help the person find ways to overcome the fear (Jones & Jones, 1928). An in-depth discussion of intervention at this level of prevention is presented in the section below entitled "Counseling Model for Working with Fearful Children." For a more in-depth discussion of the concepts outlined here as part of the primary prevention model, please see Robinson and Rotter (1991) as listed in the reference section.

The Foundations for Successful Coping

Children who have confidence in their ability to master and control events and challenges in their lives are less vulnerable to fear. These children have a sense of personal power. In contrast, a child who feels helpless in the face of danger is vulnerable to fears (Craske, 1997).

Children's perception of their power will influence their decision to fight to overcome the fear object or try to escape the fear object through flight. Children's sense of power in relationship to their environment and their ability to assess accurately the power of the fear object is central in learning to cope with fear. A realistic or unrealistic assessment of one's personal power with regard to a fear object can mean the difference between successful coping behaviors or a feeling of helplessness.

Power can be seen not only as an internal force, but also as external – the allies that the child brings to bear on the fear object. These allies can be parents, teachers, peers, or anyone with whom the child has built a supportive relationship. Indeed, the way adults around the child handle stressful situations and traumatic events can affect the level of fear response on the part of the child (Linares, Heeren, Bronfman, Zuckerman, Augustyn, & Tronick, 2001)

Related to power are three important constructs: self-worth, security and control. These concepts are explained in more detail below.

Self-Worth

Children who feel good about themselves, hold themselves in high esteem, and experience success in meeting normal developmental tasks have well-developed concepts of self-worth. Based on this success identity, they are more likely to have the confidence needed to explore and attempt new strategies to overcome fears. A child with a positive sense of self-worth will perceive a move to a new school as an opportunity to meet new friends and experience new challenges.

Security

Children who have adults in their lives that care for and encourage them develop a sense of security. Because they have allies on whom they can count, they are able to build supportive interpersonal relationships with peers and adults. Children who are secure have little difficulty reaching out to others when faced with new situations and changes in their lives.

Control

Children who are given some autonomy in decision-making learn that they have a degree of control over their lives. They learn to assess their strengths and weaknesses and accept that coping with dilemmas in life is a natural part of growing up. Faced with a potentially daunting situation, such as shopping in an open-air market, children with a sense of control enter with confidence that they can succeed in mastering a new environment.

Implications for the Educator

This concept of the relationship between personal power in the face of a child's normal fears and a child's estimate of self-worth, security and control has important implications for the educator in helping children cope with normal fears as well as helping children whose overreaction to fear is self-defeating and impeding normal growth and development. An understanding teacher can make a significant difference in the ability of children to cope with normal fears or a specific crisis evoking a fear response. Thus, it is important that the teacher become aware of those common fears that children experience at each stage of development.

Signs of Fear and Stress

The signs or symptoms of stress that children manifest are clues to teachers about the children's ability to cope with a specific fear or general anxiety. Some of these signs are obvious while others are covert and require some investigation. Educators and counselors should be aware of the signs of fear and stress in their students, preferably before the crisis stage is reached. As in most things, prevention is more sensible than remediation.

As part of a project to identify teachers' perceptions of children's fears, a group of schoolteachers was asked to identify the outward signs of fears and stress in their students (Williams, 1989). The respondents generated an enormous number of signs that can be categorized into seven groups. Following is a summary of these findings:

- *Physical manifestations*: Illnesses (real or imagined), head and stomach aches, frequent urination, tiredness, loss of weight, aches and pains, profuse sweating.
- *Emotional reactions*: Crying, sensitivity, stammering, "hair trigger" responses, irritability, excess giggling, easily startled, sudden changes of expression, general unrest.
- *Work habits*: Poor presentation of work, doodling, daydreaming, frequent absence, disorganization, cheating, sleeping in class, not staying on task, lack of concentration.
- *Nervous manifestations*: Ticks, nail biting, blinking, hair chewing, sucking fingers, fidgeting, rocking motions, chewing clothing.
- *Misbehavior and aggression*: Violence, breaking pencils, loss of temper, striking out, bad language, violent drawings, quarreling, uncontrollable rage, bullying, destructiveness, theft.

- *Attention seeking*: Immature behavior, seeking approval, demands for attention, making up bizarre stories, continuous questioning, clinging to teacher, acting out, faking injuries.
- *Self-destructive tendencies*: Suicide threats, suicide attempts, not caring what happens, self-denigration, alcohol and/or drug abuse.

The Development of Children's Fears and Stress

Due to the fact that a fear object frightens one child but the same object does not frighten another child gives rise to the individuality of perceptions of a given fear object's power to elicit a fearful response. Fear, then, must be understood on an individual basis; yet, children exhibit many of the same types of responses to fear objects and report many similar fear objects at (or around) the same age. Thus, there must also be some common phenomenon that children in general share regarding fear.

The controversy of heredity versus environment is always an issue in examining the development of attributes in children (Kagan, 1986). Stevenson-Hinde and Shouldice (1995) have been engaged in a longitudinal study of children from birth to age eight. Their findings suggest that children may have some inherent predisposition toward fearfulness. Some children are much more prone to fearful behaviors from birth than other children. They also noted that over a period of eight years some children who were more fearful at birth became less so and some who were less fearful became more so. This suggests that, although there may be a hereditary link involved in the development of fear, environmental factors also play a large part in the development of children's fears. Although Kagan's research suggests that some children will be prone to react more to fear objects, it is generally agreed that all children will exhibit fears and, while many are transitory in nature, the fears appear at about the same age for most children (Craske, 1997; Jersild, Markey, & Jersild, 1933; Morris & Kratochwill, 1983; Robinson, et. al, 1986).

Parental modeling can also play an important part in the development of children's fears. The parent who overreacts to stressful or fear-invoking stimuli can influence the development of fear and stress in children (Muris, Steerneman, Merckelbach, & Meesters, 1996). In a recent study, researchers found that the level of anxiety of mothers of children ages three to six years old who were exposed to community violence experienced less chance of behavior problems if the mothers were able to mediate their own anxiety (Linares et al., 2001).

In addition, traumatic events can adversely affect children (Figley & McCubbin, 1983; Terr, 1981; Trautman, 1987). A traumatic event in a child's life can lead to fear-related problems that interfere with the child's normal functioning. Certainly, the exact link between fear-related disorders and traumatic events can be argued, but there is ample support for the general connection (Honig, 1986). These traumatic events may be public knowledge such as earthquakes or hurricanes or more private trauma such as physical, sexual or psychological abuse.

Increasing evidence exists that video games may add to children's stress and fear. A by-product of the concern over the violence in video games has been the discovery that anxiety and increased levels of fear may accompany the increase in violence in children. Unlike television, children become engaged in the world of the video game that takes on a participatory realism unlike children's unstructured play. For the young child, the realism and graphic detail of the violence represented in the game can trigger fears, and the constant demand to perform during some software programs increases the level of stress.

The Role of the Teacher and Counselor

Children who have been exposed to traumatic events or are preoccupied with the stressors or fears they are attempting to cope with are not fully engaged in learning. Therefore, a role of the teacher may be to find ways to integrate activities and resources into the classroom that will help all children cope with fears and stress. A developmental approach is the optimal way of helping children develop coping behaviors to interact with the fears and stressors of their environment in a positive way so as to enhance growth. A developmental approach considers the nature of child development, the tasks to be accomplished, and the skills needed for continued growth.

Assessing the school environment to identify sources of fears and stress that can be eliminated or modified is an important place to begin. Then activities can be incorporated into the curriculum which enhance students' feelings of self-worth, security and control.

For example, activities that help students learn more about their own interests and personal strengths can enhance self-confidence and feelings of self-worth. Security can be increased with activities to facilitate the development of communication skills and positive interpersonal relationships with peers and adults. Problem-solving skills and strategies that enhance decision-making can increase children's sense of control in coping with the normal demands of fears and stressors in their environment.

Counseling Model for Working with Fearful Children

The counseling model proposed in this book is a four-phase counseling scheme that incorporates the ideas of security, control, and self-worth into the model of coping. During the first phase, the counselor focuses on establishing a positive relationship, providing cathartic release, exploring the child's world and validating the child's fear with the goal of self-exploration for the child. The second phase of the model deals with assessment where the counselor defines the fear in relationship to trauma or disaster and/or the constructs of security, control, and self-worth. The goal of this stage is self-understanding. As part of the third phase, the counselor generates and implements a plan of action to assist the child in order to deal with the fear object and increase the child's sense of security, self-worth and control. The fourth and final phase looks at the impact of counseling strategies in reducing the child's distress and evaluates whether or not the interventions need to be repeated with focus on another area or another fear. The types of techniques recommended for use in each of the phases are included in a quick reference format as part of Appendix I-A. The counseling model presented here is a summary of the counseling model included as Appendix I-A. Please refer to Appendix I-A for a more in-depth discussion of the model and for the quick guide that may be copied for easy reference.

Coping Through Self-Expression

Specific opportunities to explore and express the fears of childhood in a supportive setting help the child learn to cope. Expression itself can provide a release for much of the tensions that stress and fear elicit. Children are often reluctant to admit to fears because our culture teaches them that they are supposed to be brave. This "fear of admitting fear" can be overcome through capitalizing on the teachable moments as they arise and providing many varied opportunities and activities for children to express their fears openly and in a nonjudgmental atmosphere. In addition, being aware of unspoken fears and giving children the opportunity to reveal their concerns may reduce the potential for a traumatic experience and avoid the development of more intense fear.

Sometimes the immediacy of a crisis incident or the overreaction of a particular child to a specific fear requires direct intervention. A fear may be disabling to the point of impeding the normal growth and development of the child. As a professional in the school setting, listening may be the most valuable service to perform. Allowing students to express their feelings and articulate their fears helps children to assess their own levels of security, control and self-worth.

Working in concert with the child's family and eliciting the support of other school professionals are further ways of offering direct help to the child. The teacher is often in the best position to notice aberrant behavior on the part of the child that may signal the need for intervention. Then, teachers can make the proper referral to the school counselor, if one is available.

If no counseling professionals are on staff at the school, it would behoove teachers and the school administration to make an assessment of the mental health facilities within the community. Being familiar with the resources of the local community can be of vital importance in assisting the child and the family.

References

Adler, J. (1999). Stress. *Newsweek, CXXXIII,* No, 24, 56-63.

American Psychiatric Association. (2000). *Diagnostic and statistical manual of mental disorders* (4th ed., text revision). Washington, DC: Author.

Burnett, G. H. (2002). Unwed teenage mothers: An ounce of prevention is worth a ton of cure. *The American Journal of Family Therapy, 30,* 57-61.

Craske, M. (1997). Fear and anxiety in children and adolescents. *Bulletin of the Menninger Clinic, 61,* A5-A36.

Croak, J., & Knox, F. (1971). A second look at adolescent fears. *Adolescence, 6,* 279-284.

Dong, Q., Yang, B., & Ollendick, T. (1994). Fears in Chinese children and adolescents and their relations to anxiety and depression. *Journal of Child Psychology and Psychiatry, 35,* 351-363.

Figley, C. R., & McCubbin, H. I. (eds.). (1983). *Stress and the family vol. 2, Coping with catastrophe.* NY: Bruner and Mazell.

Franklin, C., & Corcoran, J. (2000). Preventing adolescent pregnancy: A review of programs and practices. *Social Work, 45* (1), 40-53.

Greydanus, D. E. (ed.). (1991). *Caring for your adolescent: Ages 12 to 21.* New York: Bantum.

Gullone, E., & King, N. (1995). The fears of youth in the 1990s: Contemporary normative data. *The Journal of Genetic Psychology, 154,* 137-153.

Hall, G. S. (1897). A study of fears. *American Journal of Psychology, 8,* 147-249.

Honig, A. S. (1986). Stress and coping in children. *Young Children,* 50-63.

Jersild, A., & Holmes, F. (1935). A study of children's fears. *Journal of Experimental Education, 2,* 109-118.

Jersild, A. T., Markey, F. U., & Jersild, C. L. (1933). Children's fears, dreams, wishes, daydreams, likes, dislikes, pleasant and unpleasant memories. *Child Development Monograph, 12.* NY: Teacher's College Press.

Jones, H. E., & Jones, M. C. (1928). Fear. *Childhood Education, 5,* 136-143.

Kagan, J. (1986). Childhood development: A longitudinal study. Paper presented at the University of South Carolina, Columbia, SC.

Kellerman, J. (1981). *Helping the fearful child.* NY: Norton.

King, N., Mietz, A., Tinney, L., & Ollendick, T. (1995). Psychopathology and cognition in adolescents experiencing severe test anxiety. *Journal of Clinical Child Psychology, 24,* 49-54.

Kirkman, C. J. & Walz, G. R. (Eds.). (2002). *Helping people cope with tragedy and grief.* Greensboro, NC: ERIC Counseling and Student Services Clearinghouse.

Linares, L. O., Heeren, T., Bronfman, E., Zuckerman, B., Augustyn, M., & Tronick, E. (2001). A mediational model for the impact of exposure to community violence on early child behavior problems. *Child Development, 72*(2), 639-652.

Maurer, A. (1965). What children fear. *Journal of Genetic Psychology, 10,* 265-277.

Muris, P., Steerneman, P., Merckelbach, H., & Meesters, C. (1996). The role of parental fearfulness and modeling in children's fear. *Behavioral Research, 14,* 265-268.

Muris, P., & Merckelbach, H. (2000). Fears, worries, and scary dreams in 4- to 12-year-old children: Their content, developmental pattern, and origins. *Journal of Clinical Child Psychology, 29*(1), 43-52.

Morris, R. J., & Kratochwill, T. R. (1983). *Treating children's fears and phobias: A behavioral approach.*New York: Pergamon.

Ollendick, T., King, N., & Frary, R. (1989). Fears in children and adolescents: Reliability and generalizability across gender, age, and nationality. *Behavioral Research, 27,* 19-26.

Ollendick, T., King, N., & Yule, W. (1994). *International handbook of phobic and anxiety disorders in children and adolescents.* NY: Plenum Press.

Plonk, K. (1999). Unpublished dissertation. A comparative analysis of the self-reported fears of academically gifted and regular education students. University of South Carolina, Columbia, SC.

Ramirez, S., & Kratochwill, T. (1997). Self-reported fears in children with and without mental retardation. *Mental Retardation, 35,* 83-92.

Robinson, E. H., Robinson, S. L., & Whetsell, M. V. (1988). The study of children's fear. *Journal of Humanistic Education and Development, 27,* 84-95.

Robinson, E. H., Robinson, S. L., Whetsell, M. V., & Weber, A. (1986, April). Fear: A developmental perspective. Presentation at the annual meeting of the American Association for Counseling and Development, Los Angeles.

Robinson, E. H., & Rotter, J. C. (1991). Children's fears: Toward a preventive model. *School Counselor, 38* (3), 187-203.

Rotter, J. C., & Robinson, E. H. (1987). Coping with fear and stress: Classroom interventions. *International Quarterly, 5(4),* 39-44.

Silverman, W., & Kurtines, W. (1996). *Anxiety and phobic disorders: A pragmatic approach.* NY: Plenum Press

Spirito, A., Francis, G., Overholser, J., & Frank, N. (1996). Coping, depression, and adolescent suicide attempts. *Journal of Clinical Child Psychology, 25* (2), 147- 155.

Stevenson-Hinde, J. & Shouldice, A. (1995). Fearful behavior, fears and worries. *Journal of Child Psychology and Psychiatry, 36,* 1027-1038.

Svensson, L., & Oest, L. (1999). Fears in Swedish children: A normative study of the Fear Survey Schedule for Children—revised. *Scandinavian Journal of Behaviour Therapy, 28*(1), 23-36.

Swanston, H. Y., Nunn, K. P., Oates, R. K., Tebbutt, J. S., & O'Toole, B. I. (1999). Hoping and coping in young people who have been sexually abused. *European Child & Adolescent Psychiatry, 8,* 134-142.

Sweatt, L., Harding, C. G., Knight-Lynn, L., Rasheed, S., & Carter, P. (2002). Talking about the silent fear: Adolescents' experiences of violence in an urban high-rise community. *Adolescence, 37*(145), 109-120.

Terr, I. C. (1981). Trauma: Aftermath: The young hostages of Chowchilla. *Psychology Today, 15(4),* 29-30.

Trautman, D. H. (1987). When disaster strikes. *International Quarterly, 5(4),* 46-48.

Williams, S. (1989). *Differences in the perceptions of children's fears: Teachers, parents, and children.* Unpublished doctoral dissertation, University of South Carolina, Columbia.

Wood, M. M. (2001). Preventing school failure: A teacher's current conundrum. *Preventing School Failure, 45* (2), 52-58.

Yule, I., Perrin, S., & Smith, P. (1999). Post-traumatic stress disorders in children and adolescents. In I. Yule (Ed.), *Post-traumatic stress disorders: Concepts and therapy*. Gloucester, England: John Wiley and Sons, Ltd.

Section 2
Fear-Specific Activities

Introduction

Fear-specific activities are those activities designed to address children's issues with a specific fear object that is typical for the child's developmental level. For instance, the number one fear of children between the ages of six and twelve years old is a fear of the dark. Therefore, an activity that addresses issues in children's lives concerning the dark is a fear-specific activity. Completing an entire unit on the topic of fears of the dark integrating art, literature, science, social studies, and math has been used successfully in the classroom to address this fear. In such a unit during science, children might examine how plants benefit the ecosystem during the night or how nocturnal animals use and adapt to the dark. As a part of social studies, children might explore different careers of individuals in public service who work during the evening such as firefighters, policemen, public transportation workers, etc. As a part of language arts, students might read, *Good Night Moon* or *Poinsettia the Pig and the Firefighters* or *Who's Afraid of the Dark*. For writing, students can do some creative writing on what they like best about nighttime or other topics. For math, students can give estimates on hours, minutes, etc. of nighttime at different times of the year.

This set of activities is not meant to be exhaustive but to provide examples. We encourage counselors and teachers to develop their own fear-specific activities or problem-based learning situations that address co-curricular learning in both academic and emotional domains.

Shadows

Fear:	The Dark
Curricular Areas:	Art, Science, Language Arts
Grades:	K-2
Size:	Full class
Time:	60-90 minutes
Purpose:	To help children cope with the fear of the dark by exploring the physical nature of shadows, the fears they feel, and how they can cope with those nighttime fears.

Outcomes:

The students will be able to:
1. Explain the physical origin of shadows;
2. Generate descriptive words about shadows;
3. Create their own drawings or paintings of shadows;
4. Identify ways of coping with shadow-related fears.

Materials:

1. Overhead or filmstrip projector (or flashlight)
2. Screen (or blank wall)
3. Large sheet of paper (or chalkboard)
4. White drawing paper
5. Black crayons or black paint and brushes

Procedures:

1. Using an overhead or filmstrip projector, have the children create shadows with their fingers and other objects, projecting them on a screen or wall, and discuss how shadows are made
2. As a group activity, write on a large sheet of paper (or chalkboard) the words children use to describe the shadows and how they feel when they see shadows at night.
3. Provide materials for the children to draw or paint a shadow on a piece of white drawing paper.
4. As a group, encourage individuals to talk about their shadow pictures. Ask them what they do at night when they see shadows. Discuss with them what they might do the next time they see a shadow at night.

Coping strategy suggestions:
      a. Turn a light on to make the shadow go away.
      b. Tell yourself it's only a shadow.
      c. Get reassurance from a sibling or parent.
      d. Turn on light to make your own shadows.

Puppets: Ghosts, Goblins and Monsters

Fear: Imaginary Creatures

Curricular Areas: Art, Music, Language Arts

Grades: K-2

Size: Full class

Time: 30 minutes

Purpose: To help children cope with the fear of imaginary creatures by transforming their own versions of nightmares or monsters into puppets.

Outcomes: *The students will be able to:*
1. Create their own puppet version of an imaginary creature;
2. Share their nightmares with other students through puppetry;
3. Identify what the children in the story or song do to cope with their fears;
4. Discuss what they can do when they have a nightmare or feel threatened by frightening creatures in the dark.

Materials: 1. Book: *There's a Nightmare in My Closet* by Mercer Mayer or Song: *"It Was All a Dream"* on the album *Tickly Toddle* by Hap Palmer
2. Construction paper
3. Glue
4. Small paper bags
5. Markers
6. Scissors

Procedures: 1. Read the story to the class or play and sing the song and discuss the coping behaviors of the characters.
2. Give the students an opportunity to share their experiences with nightmares or imaginary creatures.
3. Provide them with materials and instructions to make their own puppet versions of night mares or monsters.
4. Allow children to interact with each other. Encourage them to provide voices for their puppets.
5. Have the children design a puppet that makes them feel safe or could rescue them from their nightmare or monster puppet.
6. Allow the children another opportunity to interact with each other using voices for their new puppets.
7. As closure to the activity, discuss with the children what they can do when they have nightmares or when they think there is a monster in the room.

Coping strategy suggestions:
    a. Get reassurance from a parent or a sibling.
    b. Turn on the light and examine the room.
    c. Surround themselves with their own stuffed animals and playthings.
    d. For nightmares, get a drink of water and reassure themselves that it was only a dream.

Fantasy Trip

Fear: Strangers, New Places

Curricular Areas: Science, Art, Social Studies, Language Arts

Grades: K-2

Size: Full class

Time: 180 minutes (several classes)

Purpose: To help children explore feelings associated with unfamiliar people and places and to realize what we can do to make unfamiliar things more familiar.

Outcomes: *The students will be able to:*
1. Identify situations and people that may be strange or unfamiliar;
2. Create an imaginary world;
3. Identify familiar and unfamiliar people and things on the school campus;
4. Discuss the people and things that were strange and are now familiar and comfortable.

Materials: 1. Book: *Where the Wild Things Are* by Maurice Sendak.
2. Clay
3. Boxes
4. Paper
5. Paint
6. Portable tape recorder
7. Blank audio tape

Procedures: 1. Introduce and read the book, *Where the Wild Things Are*. Discuss Max's trip to an imaginary world and the strange creatures he found there.
2. Expand the discussion by asking the students to talk about:
   a. If they'd like to travel in space;
   b. If they wonder what other worlds and the people who live there might be like;
   c. What it would be like to be a tiny bug or giant in the world;
   d. What it would be like to be on the bottom of the ocean and what kinds of life would be found there.
3. Have the children make a model of an imaginary world. They could use clay, boxes, paper, and paint to create a world different from ours. They could describe people and animals that live there—what they eat, where and how they live, and so on. Allow time to share and discuss their world.
4. Take a walk around the school campus. Look for familiar and unfamiliar people, places and things. When an unfamiliar person, place or thing is encountered, examine, explain or introduce the students to the unfamiliar thing in order to familiarize them with it. Tape record what the children think and feel about what they see. Listen to the recording in the classroom and discuss how unfamiliar things become familiar.

What's That Sound?

Fear:	The Dark
Curricular Areas:	Science, Language Arts
Grades:	K-3
Size:	Full class
Time:	15 minutes
Purpose:	To teach children that the sounds they hear are often identifiable and come from safe sources
Outcomes:	*The students will be able to:* 1. Listen for and identify everyday sounds; 2. Recognize that things that go "bump in the night" are often the same noises that they ignore during the daytime.
Materials:	1. Flashlight 2. Classroom objects (i.e, fans, small appliances, clocks, computers, classroom pet in its cage) that often make slight noises
Procedures:	1. During a relatively quiet time of the day, turn off all the lights in the classroom. 2. Ask the children to sit as still as possible and listen for sounds. 3. After listening for about three minutes, have them describe and imitate the sounds that they heard. 4. Have the other children guess the origin of the sound. 5. Repeat this process at other times of the day in other rooms that may have different sounds. 6. Encourage the children to repeat this activity with a parent in various rooms of their home including their bedroom in order to identify some of the noises they hear when trying to go to sleep at night.

Send the Monster Packing

Fear:	Monsters, The Dark
Curricular Areas:	Art, Language Arts
Grades:	K-4
Size:	Full class
Time:	30 minutes
Purpose:	To help children cope with the fear of monsters in the dark and to visualize the monster packing up and leaving for good.

Outcomes:
The students will be able to:
1. Make a conscious effort to alleviate their fear of the monster;
2. Develop a ritual to cope with this fear the next time that it is encountered.

Materials:
1. Old pillowcases
2. Red polka dots made of felt material
3. Elmer's glue
4. Small twigs that have no sharp edges
5. Pre-cut geometric shapes representing pants, shirts and cookies of all sizes. In addition, labels from peanut butter, jelly, or other canned goods may be used.

Procedures:
1. Put all the materials in the center of a circle and allow the children to look at the materials.
2. Let them ask questions about the materials.
3. Tell them the following story about a monster who left for good:

> Once upon a time, there was a HUGE monster who loved the dark. He stayed in the prince's bedroom night after night. He grew tired of staying there because the prince was scared of how he looked. The monster wanted so much to go home to his monster family but didn't have anything that he could use for packing his clothes! One day, the prince turned off the light and asked him, "What would it take to send you packing?" The monster said, "I was waiting for you to ask so that I might trouble you for a sack in order to pack up my clothes!" The prince looked around and found a sack and helped the monster pack. Then, the monster told the prince, "I'm sorry that I scared you, and I'm glad to be going home to my monster family!" (In this story, the children may participate by describing what the monster looked like and what he/she thinks he will need to pack in order to go home.)

4. Give children time to comment, then say, "I think that the monster needs to take this! (Show the felt pants and put them in the sack) Then ask, "Do you think this will help him find his way home?"
5. Have the children make their own sacks using what they believe the monster would need in order to go home.
6. Questions for discussion:
    a. Do you get afraid when the monster won't go home?
    b. What can you do the next time you are afraid of the monster?
    c. Can you send him packing?

The questions may help children cope the next time they see a monster in the dark – they may just try to send him packing!

Flashlight

Fear:	The Dark
Curricular Areas:	Science, Art
Grades:	K-4
Size:	Full class
Time:	90 minutes
Purpose:	To help alleviate students' fears of the dark and nighttime.
Outcomes:	*The students will be able to:* 1. Realize that their room does not change in the dark; 2. Fall asleep with less apprehension.
Materials:	1. Paper 2. Markers 3. Clipboard 4. Flashlights
Procedures:	1. Discuss with students the different reasons why they are afraid of the dark. 2. Have the students draw a colorful picture of their room with as much detail as possible. 3. Have the students place their illustrations on a clipboard and talk about what specifically they are afraid of while pointing to it on the picture (i.e., monsters in the closet, things under the bed, or something else hidden in the picture). 4. Pass out the flashlights. 5. Turn off the lights but leave the door cracked to let in some light then ask the students to turn on their flashlights and look at their picture again. 6. Ask if anything has changed in their picture or in the room. 7. Have children turn off the flashlights and eliminate as much of the external light as possible then have the children turn the flashlights on again. 8. Discuss if anything has changed this time. 9. Have children take their pictures home and hang them on a wall in their bedroom with parental permission. 10. Repeat this same activity in their bedroom at home to see if anything changes in their room as it gets darker and have children report back

Alphabet of Feelings

Fear: Any Fear

Curricular Areas: Language Arts, Health/Science

Grades: K-4

Size: Small group

Time: 30 minutes

Purpose: To help students understand feelings related to fear and stress and to recognize ways of coping with situations that trigger these feelings.

Outcomes: *The students will be able to:*
1. Demonstrate the facial expression and body gestures associated with a specific feeling;
2. Tell about a situation that triggered a fearful or stressful feeling;
3. Name helpful ways to cope with the feeling and situation.

Materials: 1. Feelings poster or pictures from a magazine or book
2. Alphabet letters

Procedures: 1. Present the letter "A" with its shape, sound and how to write it (either printed or in cursive depending on age level).
2. Show a picture of someone who looks "Afraid."
3. Introduce the feeling of being afraid.
4. Ask students to show how their face and body looks when they feel afraid.
5. Ask students to think about a time when they were afraid and ask, "What happened that made you feel afraid?"
6. With each situation named by a student, ask them what they did that was helpful in each situation and solicit ideas from other students about what could be done in a particular situation.
7. Feeling words that can be explored on other days: Frightened, Nervous, Scared, Terrified, and Worried.

Nighttime

Fear:	Nighttime, The Dark
Curricular Areas:	Science, Social Studies, Language Arts
Grades:	K-5
Size:	Full class or small group
Time:	Varies
Purpose:	To help children learn about the Earth's rotation and the process of night.

Outcomes:

The students will be able to:
1. Explain the Earth's rotation and what happens to the sun when they can no longer see it;
2. Learn about children on the other side of the Earth who are having daytime when they are having nighttime.

Materials:
1. Globe
2. Light
3. Books, videos, and internet resources that depict children from other cultures who experience day while they experience night

Procedures:
1. Ask students what happens to the sun at night and discuss these ideas.
2. Using the globe and the light conduct a demonstration of the Earth's rotation and the way that the sun's light travels across the planet.
3. Have students identify specific regions or countries that have daylight while they have nighttime.
4. Ask students what they know about these different regions or countries.
5. Use children's literature, non-fiction books, videos, and Internet resources to teach children about life in these other cultures, focusing on children their age.
6. If possible, arrange for a pen pal partnership.

The Wonderful World of Ants

Fear: Insects, Ants

Curricular Areas: Science, Language Arts

Grades: K-5

Size: Full class

Time: 90 minutes (split into smaller sessions as needed)

Purpose: To encourage children to realize that insects have a place in the ecological structure and exist in orderly societies similar to humans.

Outcomes: *The students will be able to:*
1. Appreciate that insects, especially ants, exist within a social order replete with role definitions and responsibilities;
2. List some of the similarities between ants and humans.

Materials: 1. Ant farm
2. Books on ants and other insects

Procedures: 1. Introduce the topic of insects and ants with a story, video, or textbook.
2. Set up the ant farm and indicate that this will be a source of observation and findings for the coming weeks.
3. Have children record their observations of the ants and attempt to have children observe ants outside building anthills and gathering food.
4. Read about the different roles and responsibilities of the ants and compare/contrast their lives with those of humans.

Superheroes

Fear: Any Fear

Curricular Areas: Language Arts, Art

Grades: K-6

Size: Full class, small group, or individual

Time: 45 minutes

Purpose: To help children deal with their fears through creative expression and fantasy.

Outcomes: *The students will be able to:*
1. Identify the problems, challenges and fears of the superheroes;
2. Discuss the various powers that superheroes hold and how they use these to address their problems, challenges, and fears;
3. Generate ways of coping with or conquering their own fears.

Materials: 1. Superhero comic books
2. Art supplies

Procedures:

1. Read stories from the comic books aloud to children or have the children select a comic book to read.
2. Ask students to identify the types of fears, problems, and challenges that the superheroes faced in the stories.
3. Discuss with students the various powers that the superheroes hold and how these powers helped the superheroes to overcome their fears, problems, and challenges.
4. Ask whether any of the students are willing to share their fears, problems, or challenges with the class and spend some time discussing these.
5. Have students identify what superpowers they would like to have. How might these help them to overcome their fears?
6. Distribute the art supplies and ask students to create their own comic books in which they are the superheroes. They should use their superpowers to overcome fears, problems, and challenges.
7. Share comic book stories with other students if students are willing in order to give other students creative solutions to their own fears and problems.

Using Children's Literature

Fear: Any Fear

Curricular Area: Language Arts

Grades: 6-8

Size: Full class

Time: 30 minutes

Purpose: To help children realize that others share the same fears and to help them cope with their fears.

Outcomes: *The students will be able to:*
1. Identify the character's fear after reading stories or books;
2. Discuss their own experiences with this fear;
3. Identify ways the character coped with his/her fear;
4. Generate ways of coping with this fear the next time it is encountered.

Materials: A story or book selected from the *Bibliography of Children's Fears* (see Appendix 1-D) or another story which addresses a childhood fear and in which the character is able to cope with his/her fear.

Procedures: 1. Allow students to choose a story, book or chapter in a book that deals with a specific fearful situation. Ask them to notice what the character is afraid of and what the character does when he/she is afraid.
2. Discuss the story with the students. Ask the students about the following:
   a. The character and what the character was afraid of;
   b. Times they have experienced a similar fear;
   c. How they felt inside when they were afraid;
   d. What the character did in the story to cope with his/her fear;
   e. What they do to help themselves when they are afraid;
   f. What they might do the next time they experience this fear.

Discussion of the stories or books is the crucial part of this activity. It provides opportunities for students to share how they would feel, think, and act in a similar situation and learn how the story's character or other peers would cope with the same situation.

Dress Up

Fear: Insects, Cockroaches

Curricular Areas: Art, Language Arts

Grades: 2-5

Size: Full class or small group

Time: 30 minutes

Purpose: To help alleviate the fear of cockroaches and other insects.

Outcomes: *The students will be able to:*
1. Lower their anxiety regarding roaches;
2. Find ways of making encounters with insects humorous rather than horrifying.

Materials: 1. Black and white outline of a cockroach
2. Markers
3. Construction paper
4. Glue

Procedures: 1. Take the outline of the cockroach and dress it up in a funny outfit including hats, hair, clothing, make-up, earrings, or shoes if desired.
2. Share the pictures with other students or members of the class.
3. Remind students that they can repeat this activity with outlines of other bugs and that the next time they see a roach to remember what the roach looks like all dressed up.

As a supplemental activity, students can write a story with their cockroach as the main character.

Moving

Fear:	Moving
Curricular Areas:	Language Arts, Math, Art, Social Studies
Grades:	3-5
Size:	Full class
Time:	120 minutes (several classes)
Purpose:	To help children express and share the common anxieties and stressors that may accompany moving to a new home.

Outcomes:

The students will be able to:
1. Identify and discuss the stressors and anxieties that families experience when moving;
2. Create a mural showing the sequence of events in moving from one home to another;
3. Build models of different kinds of houses used around the world;
4. Use maps to calculate distances between places.

Materials:

1. Mural paper
2. Crayons, paint or markers
3. Materials for building house models, such as clay, straws, wooden sticks, sugar cubes, cardboard, glue, etc.

Procedures:

1. Discuss with the children:
   a. Reasons why families move;
   b. How a family gets ready for a move;
   c. Problems a family faces when they move;
   d. Various ways furniture and belongings are moved from one place to another;
   e. The students' experiences with moving;
   f. How it feels to be in a new neighborhood without any friends;
   g. What you can do to make friends in a new place;
   h. How you can help a new child who moves into your area.
2. Students can break up into small groups to work on one of the following activities or the activity's length can be extended so that every student can experience each activity.
   a. *Murals*: Create a mural showing the sequence of events in moving from one home to another (i.e., garage sales, packing, traveling, etc.). Dialogue can be added to the characters shown.
   b. *Models*: Build models of different kinds of houses used around the world, such as apartment buildings, frame houses, igloos, mud huts, straw houses, stone houses, etc. Have the children create backdrops behind the models, showing the countryside that would be found around the dwellings.
   c. *Map Math*: Have the students calculate the distances between cities and countries around the world. Have students figure out whose hometown is farthest away from the school and whose hometown is the closest.
   d. *Hometown Sharing*: Have students give reports on their hometowns, comparing and contrasting them with where they are living now.
   e. Be sure to take time to share and discuss projects.

Writing About Fears

Fear:	Any Fear
Curricular Area:	Language Arts
Grades:	3-5
Size:	Full class
Time:	60 minutes
Purpose:	To help children express and share their fears and coping strategies through writing.
Outcomes:	*The students will be able to:* 1. Create stories and poetry about fears; 2. Share their stories with their peers; 3. Identify alternate modes of coping with their fears.
Materials:	1. Composition paper 2. Pencil or pen

Procedures:

Activity One: Story Starters

Give the students one or all of the following topic sentences to begin short stories:
1. "Everybody is afraid sometimes. I remember when..."
2. "The scariest place I've ever been was..."
3. "I am a furry monster hiding in a child's dark closet. I feel..."

Activity Two: Story Building

1. Students choose an object or noun and make up a group story about it. The following sequence is an example that could easily lead to a story about haunted houses:
   a. Student 1: "I see a house."
   b. Student 2: " The house is red."
   c. Student 3: "The red house is spooky."
   d. Student 4: "The spooky, red house has spider webs in the window."
2. Students can continue with their own story.

Activity Three: Cinquains

1. A cinquain is a five line poem with a two-syllable word on the first and last lines and 4, 6 and 8 syllables on the second, third and fourth lines. An example follows:

Nighttime	2 syllables
Monsters, scary	4 syllables
Hiding, jumping, laughing	6 syllables
Come out in my bedroom at night	8 syllables
Daytime	2 syllables

After each of these writing activities, allow time to share the stories or poetry and discuss alternate means of coping with the fears expressed in the writing.

The Worry Game

Fear:	New School
Curricular Area:	Social Studies
Grades:	3-8
Size:	Full class
Time:	30 minutes
Purpose:	To help children realize that other students share anxieties about being in a new school setting and help them cope with those fears.

Outcomes:

The students will be able to:
1. Identify some worries associated with being in a new school setting;
2. Make decisions about coping strategies to deal with new school settings.

Materials: None

Procedures:

1. Divide the group into two teams, the Worriers and the Doers. The task of the Worrier team is to suggest things that might go wrong, be scary or cause worry on the first day of school. The task of the Doer team is to suggest solutions to the problems posed by the Worrier team members. If the problem is something for which there is no solution, then the Doers must suggest how a student could make the best of it.
2. Begin the game with the sentence: *"Tomorrow is your first day in a new school."*
3. Have the first Worrier team member make a suggestion of what might go wrong, be scary or cause worry. Collaboration is encouraged.
4. Have the first Doer team member provide a suggestion or decision to overcome the worry. Again, collaboration is encouraged.
5. If the Doer can make a reasonable suggestion (the teacher can be the judge), then the Doer team gets a point. If not, then the Worrier team gets a point. Continue on until all team members have had a chance to articulate a concern or a solution.
6. If time permits, have the teams switch roles. The team with the most points wins.

Book of Blessings

Fear:	Any Fear
Curricular Areas:	Social Studies, Language Arts, Art
Grades:	3-8
Size:	Full class
Time:	60 minutes
Purpose:	To help students learn what they possess to conquer fears.

Outcomes:

The students will be able to:
1. Draw and assemble pictures of what they have to help them through fearful situations;
2. Keep and post pictures as a reminder of the resources that they possess in order to conquer fears.

Materials:

1. Small (4X4) square pieces of paper
2. Crayons or colored pencils
3. Hole punch
4. Colored yarn

Procedures:

1. Begin discussion of what helps the students cope with fear and how we all have ways to help through fearful situations.
2. Discuss what fears are most common among these students.
3. Ask class to draw out what they have to help them manage their fears. For example, students may draw out family, friends, objects, favorite places, etc.
4. Ask students to make the drawings colorful in order to celebrate the ways they have to help them through fears. Punch holes in the upper left corner of the paper and thread yarn though the holes.
5. Ask students to place these in an area that they will see frequently in order to remind them of all the ways they have to help them cope with fear.

Washing Away Fear

Fear:	Any Fear
Curricular Areas:	Art, Language Arts
Grades:	3-8
Size:	Full class
Time:	45 minutes
Purpose:	To help children draw their fears and use rituals as a way to cope with them.

Outcomes:

The students will be able to:
1. Identify a fear object;
2. Talk about the way that fears make us feel;
3. Figure out ways to cope with the fear;
4. Realize that they are in control of how they respond to their fears.

Materials:

1. Sidewalk chalk
2. Cup of water

Procedures:

1. Have children proceed to a sidewalk or other area where they may draw using sidewalk chalk.
2. Ask students to picture a fear in their mind's eye and draw what it looks like using the chalk.
3. Walk around and look at the fears of other students.
4. Start a discussion on what fears are and how they make us feel.
5. Talk about ways to cope with fears including symbolically getting rid of them.
6. Have students identify their preferred method of coping with fears.
7. Take a glass of water and say, "You will not scare me anymore because…" (and fill in the blank with the method of coping that the child selected).
8. Let children dump the water on their own drawing to make the fear disappear.

Bully Busting

Fear: Bullies

Curricular Areas: Language Arts, Social Studies

Grades: 4-8

Size: Full class

Time: 50 minutes

Purpose: To help children realize that others may share the same fear of being bullied and how they can work together to overcome this fear while also recognizing the possible damage and loss of safety involved in bullying.

Outcomes: *The students will be able to:*
1. Identify some of the feelings surrounding being bullied;
2. Discuss personal fears about being bullied;
3. Consider alternatives to bullying and to acting as a bystander;
4. Identify ways of coping and handling bullies.

Materials: None

Procedures:
1. Select two students to engage in a role-playing activity where one student is bullying another student.
2. Have the student chosen as the bully taunt the other child when no one is around and have the other child run from the bully.
3. Repeat the above scene with one or two bystanders who do nothing to help the child being bullied.
4. Engage in a third role-play where one (or more) of the bystanders intervenes to help the child being bullied.
5. Discuss the role-play with the students asking them such questions as the following:
   a. What is bullying?
   b. Why is it dangerous?
   c. How did the child feel in the first scene when no one was around?
   d. What would you have done in a similar situation with no one to help you?
   e. Comparing the first and second scenes, is it better to become involved in the situation or ignore the situation?
   f. How do bullies feel?
   g. What could the characters do differently?
   h. What can you do to discourage bullying?

Shelter from the Storm

Fear:	Storms
Curricular Areas:	Science
Grades:	4-8
Size:	Full class
Time:	30 minutes
Purpose:	To help children cope with fears of thunderstorms and lightning and appreciate how animals in nature find security during storms.
Outcomes:	*The students will be able to:* 1. Express their fears in a group setting; 2. Discuss their past experiences with storms; 3. Explain how animals in nature handle storms; 4. Generate ways to cope with this fear the next time it is encountered.
Materials:	Small plastic or rubber farm animals

Procedures:	1. Allow each child to select one or two animals that they like for this exercise.
	2. Ask them to imagine what each animal does when a storm approaches.
	3. Have children act out the body movements or behaviors of the animals while seeking a secure location.
	4. Discuss the actions of the animals in preparing for the storm including the following:
	    a. What kind of shelter does the animal prefer?
	    b. How does this compare with the type of shelters that students have during a storm?
	    c. What natural characteristics do the animals have that enable them to cope with every storm?
	    d. What does the animal do during storms?
	    e. What do students do during storms?
	    f. What does the animal do after a storm?
	    g. What do the children do after a storm?

Fear Is Not My Bag

Fear: Any Fear

Curricular Areas: Language Arts, Art

Grades: 6-8

Size: Full class

Time: 60 minutes

Purpose: To express fears and learn different ways to cope with them.

Outcomes: *The students will be able to:*
1. Identify a fear or fears that they have;
2. Learn to communicate with others about their fears;
3. Discuss different coping strategies that they use or have tried.

Materials:
1. Magazines
2. Glue
3. Scissors
4. Paper Bags
5. Markers
6. Paper

Procedures:
1. Give each student a paper bag and ask him or her to use the magazines to create a fear collage on the outside of their bag.
2. Have students use paper and markers to draw how they make themselves feel better when they are scared or what they use in order to cope with their fears. Place these inside of the bag.
3. Have students share their fear bags with other students as a way to normalize fears and hear other students' coping strategies.

Yes, You Can!

Fear: Test Anxiety

Curricular Areas: Language Arts, Math, Science, Social Studies

Grades: 6-8

Size: Full class

Time: 30 minutes

Purpose: To help children cope with test anxiety and fears of failure.

Outcomes: *The students will be able to:*
1. Identify certain test-taking methods that may help them to relax;
2. Imagine the test-taking situation and a positive way of coping;
3. Generate a way of coping with the anxiety the next time it is encountered.

Materials: None

Procedures:
1. Discuss with students certain methods for success in test taking including the following:
   a. Start with questions/problems where you know the answers. Move purposefully and quickly through the test to answer those that you know while circling the ones that you don't know.
   b. Take brief breaks that include several deep breaths to relax, clear your mind, and refocus.
   c. Know that some tests have two answers that are right, but one answer is better than another. To eliminate an answer, look for words like always and never. The correct answers will usually have softer wording such as most, many, or several.
   d. Allow time to recheck your answers but don't panic and change many answers because your first answer is usually correct.
   e. Another strategy is to pretend that the test is a practice test and isn't for a grade. This helps to alleviate much of the anxiety that students feel when taking the test because they want a good grade
2. After this, do a relaxation session where the students imagine that it is the night before the test. What have you done to prepare? Have you thought of associations or memory devices to help you remember the material? Are you cramming? Have the students imagine that they are listening to their favorite music, relaxing, and going to bed early. Then have the students imagine that they are waking up the next morning well rested and ready. Be sure to have the students envision eating a good breakfast that will provide energy and brainpower. As the students eat breakfast, have them say, "Yes, I CAN do well on this test. I CAN pass it, and I CAN do it." It is important to remain in a positive frame of mind to reduce anxiety when taking the test.
3. Discuss how it felt to engage in the visualization activity.
4. Have the students try some of the techniques discussed the next time they take a test and follow-up with asking what, if any, worked for them.

A Little Night Music

Fear:	Being Home Alone
Curricular Area:	Music
Grades:	6-8
Size:	Full class
Time:	30 minutes
Purpose:	To help children feel safe and comfortable when home alone after school or into the evening.

Outcomes: *The students will be able to:*
1. Feel safe when home alone;
2. Cope with the anxiety and stress of being alone;
3. Prevent unnecessary worrying through activities that help pass the time.

Materials: Some CD or tape selections with relaxing sounds such as waterfalls, rain forests, birds and waves. Encourage students to bring in a few of their favorite relaxing tapes or CDs to class.

Procedures:

1. Have students close their eyes and sit in a relaxed position with their hands dropped gently to their sides, sitting comfortably in a chair or on the floor. Some students may want to lie down on the floor and close their eyes.
   Ask students to clear their minds, relax, and concentrate on their breathing using the deep-breathing technique of taking a deep breath, holding it while counting one then two then three, and exhaling slowly on the count of one, two, three and four.
2. Next, have students imagine a safe and special place that is theirs and theirs alone. It could be a beach, their room, their backyard, or any place where they feel secure. What does this place look like? What do you see, touch, hear and feel? Imagine what is in this most sacred and special place. You are alone in this place, and it will always be yours alone. In this place, imagine that you hear your favorite CD or tape. Be certain that this is a tape or CD that you can listen to at any time in your home.
3. After the first visualization, take students through the second visualization: Imagine that you are opening the door to your house and entering it alone. No one is home, and it is very quiet. It is later in the day and beginning to get dark outside. You feel the need to relax and listen to your music. You turn on your music and travel to the special place that you imagined a few minutes ago. You check to make sure that all doors are locked, there is nothing on the stove, the TV is off, the iron is off, and the answering machine is on. It's only you in this place, and you are more relaxed with each deep breath. Relax and enjoy how wonderful it feels to be safe here and relaxed. This is your time to relax before you have to do your homework or your chores. Take the time to name this special place of yours and remember this name any time you want to relax. It will come to you, and you will instantly begin to relax. You will remember your special place and can be there any time you need to be there. It will comfort you each time you put on your special music and travel to your special place. Because this is your place, no one else but you can go there. I want you to think of this beautiful place that is yours and yours alone. I'm going to count down from 10, and as I do, you will begin to become more aware of your surroundings, the noises and the people, and open your eyes when I reach 0. You will remember how to relax when you put on your special music to remind you of your special place. 10, 9, 8, 7...

4. Tell the students as they practice more and more, they will be able to relax at a moment's notice. If they listen to the same tape, it will help them to practice and push away the fear and uncertainty of being alone. It will give the students a feeling of comfort and security in knowing they can be by themselves.

"Real-Life" Fiction Writing

Fear:	Any Fear
Curricular Area:	Language Arts
Grades:	6-8
Size:	Full class
Time:	Several periods
Purpose:	To help students express and share anxieties and fears they may have experienced and explore alternative means of coping with them.
Outcomes:	*The students will be able to:*

The students will be able to:
1. Describe in written form a real, fearful situation that they have encountered in their lives;
2. Share their experiences with their peers;
3. Fictionalize their real-life experiences in short-story form;
4. Devise alternative means of coping with fear-inducing situations.

Materials:
1. Paper
2. Pencil or pen

Procedures:
1. Assign students the task of writing down in detail the most frightening thing that has ever happened to them. Give examples of the kinds of things that may have happened to you or to others that you know about. Have the students discuss their own experiences as a pre-writing activity.
2. Share the real life stories with classmates the next day. Have students read their stories and ask questions of them to obtain further details. Allow enough time for all the students to share their stories.
3. Choose one real-life story and, as a class, try to fictionalize the account as a model, following these steps:
      a. Make up names for the characters, describe what they look like, how they talk, where they are from, how old they are, etc. Decide on a point-of-view from which the story will be told.
      b. Describe the setting in detail, the time of year, the climate, etc.
      c. Explore plot alternatives, embellishing the story imaginatively with fictionalized details. Explore different resolutions of the problems encountered and choose the best solution.
4. Break the class into groups of 3 or 4 and have the group members brainstorm fictionalizations of each others' stories, following the model outlined above. Encourage group efforts to create exciting story lines.
5. Have each student write his own short story based on the fictionalized account of a real fearful event in his/her life.
6. Share the short stories with the entire class, either by duplicating and distributing them or having each student read his/hers to the class.

What Ifs...?

Fear:	Any Fear
Curricular Area:	Language Arts
Grades:	6-8
Size:	Full class
Time:	50 minutes
Purpose:	To help students understand the sources of anxiety and stress and generate ways to cope with setbacks and failures.
Outcomes:	*The students will be able to:* 1. Identify situations that may be sources of anxiety and stress; 2. Examine and describe a time when they tried something and failed; 3. Examine and describe a time when they were frightened but took action and succeeded; 4. Discuss what they learned about trying, failing and coping with similar situations.
Materials:	1. Chalkboard or large sheet of newsprint 2. Marker 3. Worksheet: "Risky Business"

Procedures:	1. Write the following questions on the chalkboard or newsprint:
	    a. What if I don't have anyone to eat lunch with?
	    b. What if I flunk the test?
	    c. What if I can't do the math homework?
	    d. What if I don't get any A's?
	    e. What if I...?
	2. Examine the "What if..." questions. Discuss how it is impossible to achieve our goals all the time without some setbacks and how sometimes we fall short of our expectations and have to muster the courage to start again.
	3. Brainstorm other "What if...?" problems/challenges. Record them on the board or newsprint.
	4. Have each student individually complete the worksheet, "Risky Business."
	5. Allow time to discuss generally situations that make one hesitate to act and some of the students' experiences in failing and succeeding in achieving their goals.

Risky Business

Describe a time when you decided that you'd rather do nothing than risk failure.

Describe a time when you took action, even though you were scared, and succeeded.

Describe a time when you tried something and failed. What did you learn from the experience?

What have you learned in general about trying, failing and gaining courage to try again?

Web Sites

The following Web sites may be helpful in understanding childhood fears. They may be used to collect further information for the reader or as resources for parents and others.

WEB SITES:

http://www.monstersbegone.com
  Fear of Monsters

http://www.geocities.com/Paris/Arc/9821/disability/schoolp
  School Phobia

http://trfn.clpgh.org/pcgc/fears
  Children's Fears—Parent and Child Guidance Center of Pittsburgh

http://www.humsci.auburn.edu/abell/timelyinfo/fears
  Dealing with Children's Fears – Auburn University

http://www.nncc.org/Parent/uc.fears
  Children's Fears – University of Iowa

Section 3
Fear-Prevention Activities

Introduction

Fear-prevention activities are those activities that promote a sense of power in children. If the children perceive that they are more powerful than the potential fear object, they respond in one way; if, on the other hand, they perceive that they are less powerful, they may respond in a very different way. Power consists of three different constructs: security, self-worth, and control. The extent to which children see that they are secure, feel of value, and act on their environment determines their general reaction to a potential fear object. Although most children at six years of age may fear the dark, those with a sense of power tend to believe they will find a way to master the situation; those without a sense of power may experience difficulty in coping.

Security is having a sense of well-being and safety based on having allies in facing the world and one's environment. Allies can be family, friends, teachers, spiritual faith, or even inanimate objects such as stuffed animals that the child can call on for help and comfort when faced with potential fear objects. Allies may help children develop strategies for defeating fear objects: they provide comfort when thinking of dealing with fear objects; they may also help to intervene and neutralize the influence of fear objects. Self-worth, in this case, is defined as having a sense of confidence that one is capable and of value. Children with feelings of self-worth approach a task with confidence of success. They believe that they can overcome obstacles because their personal resources are great. Control involves having a sense of acting on the environment, of exercising influence over one's life and the things that happen in life.

These three constructs empower children and help them approach tasks and obstacles in life. Children who have adults in their lives who care for and encourage them and children who have the skills to make friends develop a sense of security that allows them to explore their world. Children who feel good about themselves develop the confidence to explore and attempt new strategies to overcome fear (Rotter & Robinson, 1987).

Brainstorming

Prevention:	Security, Control
Curricular Areas:	Social Studies, Language Arts
Grades:	K-2
Size:	Full class
Time:	20 minutes
Purpose:	To help students develop critical thinking skills and recognize that there are many solutions to a situation or many ways of doing the same thing.

Outcomes: *The students will be able to:*
1. Generate many solutions or ideas for the same situation;
2. Recognize that different people approach a situation in a variety of ways.

Materials:
1. Clock or watch with second hand
2. Chart or board

Procedures:
1. Explain to the students that there are many ways of doing the same thing. In this activity, you would like them to suggest as many solutions to a situation as possible within the time limit set. Tell them that thinking of as many things as possible in a certain period of time is called "Brainstorming."
2. Allow about 3-4 minutes for each topic. Select two or three topics from the suggestions below. (The remaining topics may be used for a second lesson on brainstorming or later as readiness exercises for other problem-solving activities).
3. The rules for brainstorming are quite simple:
   - Students are to suggest (in an orderly fashion) as many solutions to the problem as they can come up with during the time set aside for suggestions.
   - During the suggestions phase, students may not comment on the quality or feasibility of the solutions. The goal is to get as many ideas out as possible.
   - Record the solutions suggested on a board or chart. Model an accepting attitude and resist any efforts on the part of students to "put down" someone else's ideas. Comment on the number of ideas and creativity that the students show.

Suggested topics for Brainstorming:
   a. How can you make friends with a new person at school?
   b. How can you decide who will be first in a game?
   c. How can you help your teacher?
   d. How can you show your mother or father you love him/her?
   e. What can you do to entertain yourself if you are home alone?
   f. What can you do during a frightening thunderstorm?
   g. What can you do if you get lost?
   h. What can you do if you are near a dog or other animal you are afraid of?

Source: Chiak, M. K., & Heron, B. J. (1980). *Games children should play.* Glenview, IL: Scott Foresman & Co.

How I've Grown

Prevention:	Self-worth
Curricular Areas:	Science, Math, Social Studies, Language Arts
Grades:	K-2
Size:	Full class, individual
Time:	60 minutes
Purpose:	To help students increase their awareness that they are unique because of their different interests and physical abilities.
Outcomes:	*The students will be able to:* 1. Identify ways they have changed and grown; 2. Name likenesses and differences between themselves and others; 3. Identify how their interests have changed; 4. Match each picture with the correct name.
Materials:	1. Bulletin board 2. Photograph of each student at a younger age 3. Yarn 4. Push pins 5. Scrapbook (optional) 6. Name cards

Procedures:	1. Ask the children to bring an earlier childhood picture (photo) of themselves and a current picture (This could be taken at school by the children or an adult).
	2. Prepare a bulletin board entitled "How I've Grown." Under the current picture, place a name card with a length of colorful yarn. Place early childhood pictures randomly on the bulletin board. Be sure children's names are on the back of their pictures.
	3. Give the children an opportunity to view the pictures and match them (younger with present day) using the yarn.
	4. Discuss what they observed and how they changed:
	    a. What differences among each other do you see?
	    b. What likenesses among each other do you see?
	    c. How have you changed from you earlier picture to now?
	    d. What did you like to do at that younger age?
	    e. What do you like to do now?

Optional: If this activity is done early in the year, the pictures can be placed in a scrapbook (one child's picture per page). Late in the year, take pictures again and make comparisons. A short story could be written about how they have changed.

Workers in the Dark

Prevention:	Control
Curricular Areas:	Social Studies, Language Arts, Reading, Art
Grades:	K-2
Size:	Full class, group, or individual
Time:	60-90 minutes
Purpose:	To help children gain a sense of security and control by realizing that many adults perform their jobs at night or in the dark.

Outcomes:

The students will be able to:
1. Identify jobs that people perform in the dark or at night;
2. Demonstrate through role playing how people who work in the dark perform their job;
3. Draw a picture or symbols of jobs people perform in the dark;
4. Match the symbol with the name of the job to which it corresponds.

Materials:

1. Heavy weight drawing paper, 5.5 x 8 inch
2. Crayons or markers

Procedures:

1. Introduce the activity by asking the children to name their parents' jobs. Ask if they can think of jobs that people perform at night or in the dark. Some possibilities include the following:

photography processor	mine worker
firefighter	deep sea diver
night security	police
astronaut	astronomer
paramedics	doctors/nurses

2. Locate (or have the children locate) books in the library about jobs that are performed in the dark or at night. Read to the children (or have them read in small groups) to find out more about those jobs. Discuss the environment they work in and why it is necessary for them to work in the dark.
3. Give each child an opportunity to role play one of the jobs and let the other students guess which job it is.
4. Provide paper and crayons or markers. Ask the students to draw a picture or symbol of the jobs discussed. Try to make sure that a picture or symbol represents each job.
5. Print (or have the students print) the name of each job on another 5.5 x 8 inch heavy piece of paper. Use the pictures and job names to play a matching game like concentration. Place all cards face down. Taking turns, turn two over at a time. If they match, that student keeps the cards. If they don't match, they are turned back over in their place. This last activity can be used for individual or small group reinforcement.

Family Pictures

Prevention:	Security, Self-worth
Curricular Areas:	Language Arts, Social Studies, Science, Art
Grades:	K-2
Size:	Full class
Time:	90-120 minutes
Purpose:	To help the students recognize that people are organized into families and that each family is unique.
Outcomes:	*The students will be able to:* 1. Name a variety of living things; 2. Classify the living things into groups or categories; 3. Draw a picture of their own family and label each member; 4. Discuss an activity that their family does together.
Materials:	1. Magazines that include as many different pictures as possible of people, animals, and plants 2. Drawing paper 3. Crayons, markers or paint 4. Chalkboard or chart 5. Glue

Procedures:	1. Discuss the meaning of the term "alive" with the children. Ask the students to name living things and list them on the board.
	 2. Provide magazines and ask the children to cut out pictures of many different living things.
	 3. Gather the children into a large group or small groups with their pictures. They can form a circle.
	 4. Ask the children to look over their pictures and decide if any of the pictures could go together in families. They may first say all the plants should go together in one family and the animals in another. Accept this but encourage finer classification, such as classifying into dog family, tree family, fish family, human family, etc.
	 5. Group the pictures according to the family classifications determined. Let each child participate.
	 6. In small groups, glue each classification or family of pictures on a large enough sheet of paper. Label each family and write one sentence about each one. Display in the room or on a bulletin board.
	 7. As a follow-up to the above activity, ask the students to draw a picture of their own family, including each member. Ask them or help them to label each member.
	 8. Gather the children into a group to talk about their families. Suggestions include the following:
	     a. Who is in your family?
	     b. Name something that your family does together.
	     c. What are families for?
	     d. Are all the families in the class alike?
	     e. What does your family do for you?
	     f. What do you do for your family?

Family Visitors

Prevention:	Security, Self-worth
Curricular Areas:	Social Studies, Language Arts
Grades:	K-2
Size:	Full class
Time:	20-30 minutes per visit
Purpose:	To help the students recognize the importance of their own family and the uniqueness of each family.
Outcomes:	*The students will be able to:* 1. Answer questions and communicate with other students about their (own) families; 2. Identify ways in which families are similar and different; 3. List reasons why families are important.
Materials:	1. Long sheet of paper (vertical or horizontal) 2. Marker

Procedures:	1. Schedule times throughout the year for each child to invite one or more members of his/her family to visit the classroom and to talk about their family. A suggestion is to send a letter home at the beginning of the year explaining the project.
	2. Before a visit, have the students draw up questions that they may wish to ask the visitors to talk about, such as the following:
	    a. The family's favorite foods
	    b. What the family does for fun
	    c. How they share responsibilities
	    d. Different places they have lived
	3. When a family visits, encourage the student and his/her family member(s) to bring pictures or other items that may represent the family.
	4. After each visit, list one or two reasons why families are important on a long paper labeled "WHY FAMILIES ARE IMPORTANT." Some examples are the following:
	
	    Families take care of each other
	    Families live together
	    Families have fun together
	    Families celebrate birthdays
	
	5. The teacher should be sure to schedule his/her own family for a visit.

Little Red Riding Hood

Prevention: Security

Curricular Areas: Reading, Language Arts

Grades: K-2

Size: Full class or small group

Time: 30 minutes

Purpose: To help children develop relationship-building and negotiating skills.

Outcomes: *The students will be able to:*
1. Express feelings through play and words
2. Acknowledge problems
3. Ask for help
4. Negotiate solutions

Materials:
1. 20 or more large cards (8" X 11") depicting a variety of animals that are friendly or ferocious and several that have mythical powers. The cards may be hand drawn or traced and cut out. On the back of the card, list some powers, strengths, secret fears, or concerns of the animal shown.
2. One red cape

Procedures:
1. Have children color the cards to become familiar with the characters.
2. Place the cards around the room in plain view following the path that the children will travel.
3. Remember this is an action adventure so assign one child at a time as Red Riding Hood, other children to play the animal characters, and others to accompany Red Riding Hood along the path. Be sure to rotate roles, so children have an opportunity to experience all the characters.
4. Select one child to play Little Red Riding Hood and invite the children to help Red Riding Hood who is afraid to go through the forest alone.
5. As Red Riding Hood travels along the path, she encounters the children acting as the animal on the card. Red Riding Hood and her friend(s) negotiate with the animals to let them pass.
6. Based on the strengths and weaknesses listed on the card, the animals may ask for help or strengths from Red Riding Hood.
7. Allow children to enter and exit Red Riding Hood's group as they wish and take on new roles.
8. Answer the following questions after the activity:
    a. How does it feel to find friends who can help?
    b. Were they surprised to learn that scary characters could be afraid of things, too?

My Safety Zone

Prevention:	Security
Curricular Areas:	Social Studies, Language Arts
Grades:	K-5
Size:	Full class
Time:	30 minutes
Purpose:	To help children learn that they have resources in order to feel safe and secure.

Outcomes:

The students will be able to:
1. Identify safe places, people, activities, and objects;
2. Realize that the safety zone can continue to grow and expand to increase security.

Materials:

1. Paper
2. Crayons or markers

Procedures:

1. Divide the paper into four quadrants.
2. Label the quadrants into the following: safe places, safe people, safe activities, and safe objects.
3. Draw pictures, symbols, or words that are representative of each area.

Note: Safety means different things to different children. Parents may be safe to one child but not to another. The same holds true for a neighbor, friend, or older child or siblings. Allow children to fill these quadrants with what they believe to be safe rather than making suggestions.

A Flag for the Kingdom

Prevention:	Control, Security
Curricular Areas:	Social Studies, Geography
Grades:	K-5
Size:	Full class or small group
Time:	50 minutes
Purpose:	To help children to explore support systems, family connections, and decision-making.

Outcomes:

The students will be able to:
1. Identify those who protect us;
2. Describe the importance of rules;
3. Demonstrate both decision-making and problem-solving skills.

Materials:

1. Construction paper
2. Crayons, paints, and markers
3. Glue
4. Magazines
5. Feathers, beads, and string

Procedures:

1. Tell the children to imagine that they are a king or a queen and must watch over their kingdom.
2. Have students name the kingdom and create a flag that is representative of the kingdom.
3. Discuss the following questions:
    a. What are the people like in your kingdom?
    b. What are the rules of the kingdom?
    c. Who protects the kingdom?
    d. How do you know when people are sad or scared in your kingdom, and what do you do to help them?
    e. How do you solve fights in your kingdom?
    f. What is the best thing about your kingdom?

Classroom Meetings

Prevention:	Control, Security, Self-Worth
Curricular Areas:	Any area
Grades:	K-8
Size:	Full class
Time:	20-40 minutes
Purpose:	To enhance communication between students and teacher, promote problem-solving skills and encourage students to take responsibility for planning classroom goals and activities.

Outcomes:

The students will be able to:
1. Identify the purpose of holding class meetings;
2. List rules and procedures for conducting class meetings;
3. Participate in a class meeting.

Materials: None

Procedures:

1. Class meetings are opportunities for students to work cooperatively to plan and make decisions about classroom rules and activities and solve problems that arise within the class.
2. Discuss the concept of class meetings with the students. Decide what the purpose of the class meetings will be and what topics will be discussed.
   Examples:
   > *Field trip ideas*
   > *Classroom chores*
   > *Rules and consequences for classroom behavior*
   > *Playground problems*
   > *Ideas for projects*
3. Suggested guidelines for class meetings:
   a. Each member should have an equal vote;
   b. A chairperson and recorder should preside at each meeting;
   c. A definite day or time each week should be set;
   d. A person must raise one's hand to be recognized;
   e. Only those things that are the business of the class should be topics for discussion;
   f. An agenda box can be set up for students to provide written agenda items;
   g. Decisions are binding, and any alternatives or changes must wait until the next meeting.
4. Suggested procedure for class meetings:
   a. Chairperson calls the meeting to order;
   b. Read meeting rules and decisions from the previous meeting;
   c. Discuss any unfinished business;
   d. Discuss only agenda items;
   e. Take a vote and let the majority rule.

The Treasure Hunt

Prevention: Self-Worth, Security

Curricular Areas: Language Arts

Grades: K-8

Size: Full class or small group

Time: 50 minutes

Purpose: To help children identify their own strengths and talents while also learning to assess the strengths and resources of others around them.

Outcomes: *The students will be able to:*
1. Identify what they like about themselves;
2. Look for good qualities in others;
3. Express feelings.

Materials:
1. A large selection of pre-selected magazine pictures that show children engaging in various activities.
2. Poster board
3. Markers
4. Glue or glue sticks
5. Scissors
6. Hat with each child's name in it

Procedures:
1. Write a list of positive qualities on the blackboard.
2. Pick one of the qualities and ask the children if they can identify someone in the class with that quality.
3. Tell the children that they are going on a treasure hunt to find things that are special about themselves, so they must look for five pictures that show something representative of themselves.
4. Paste these pictures on the poster board.
5. Have children write under the picture what they see in the picture that reminds them of themselves.
6. Allow children to select a name from the hat and find one quality from the list on the blackboard that fits the child whose name they drew.
7. Write the quality on the slip of paper and give it to the child.
8. Ask that child if he/she thought that he/she possessed that quality. Encourage students to write these qualities along with the others on their poster board.

ESL Activities

High Risk: Security, Control, Self-worth

Curricular Area: English as a Second Language (ESL)

Grades: K-8

Size: Individual

Time: Varies

Purpose: To help allay the fears of non-English speaking students in the environment of the school and in the community.

Outcomes: *The students will be able to:*
1. Relax and be calm in the school environment;
2. Begin to enter into the life of the school;
3. Begin to construct positive social relationships with peers.

Materials: See individual activities below.

Procedures: *The Non-English Speaking Child:* One of the most frightening experiences for children is to enroll at a new school in which the language of instruction is unfamiliar to the student. If the child's teachers do not know the language of the child, it can be even more stressful for the child and a source of frustration for the adults as well since language cannot be used as a mediator between the child and his/her fears. The child placed in such a seemingly hostile environment will most likely feel insecure, will probably experience a loss of control over his/her life, and will possibly lose a substantial portion of his/her sense of self-worth since he/she will not be able to function at the level that he/she had attained in the past. The following procedures may be able to alleviate some of the deleterious effects of this unpleasant experience:

1. *Security Blankets:* Find out from the parents what conveys the notion of warmth and acceptance within the culture of the child. It may be physical contact (hugs), facial expressions, food, or any number of culturally appropriate behaviors or objects. Whatever it is, make sure that you are aware of it and can demonstrate it to the child.
2. *Peer Power:* If there are other students within the class or within the school who speak the language of the child it will increase his/her sense of security. Even if there is no one who speaks the language of the child, select an especially friendly and outgoing student to be the newcomer's special "buddy."
   a. Have the peer helper show the newcomer the layout of the school, explain the school schedule and routine and act as an interpreter between school personnel and the child, if he/she speaks the child's language.
   b. It is a good idea to develop a peer helper program to train a cadre of students to act as peer facilitators. Have the helpers brainstorm ideas about what it was like to be new and what kinds of things they needed when they were newcomers with little or no language skills. Make sure that they understand that they are to help acclimate the new students so that they can begin to do things for themselves and that they are not expected to do everything for the newcomers on a sustained basis.

3. *Pictures as Words:* If there is no one in the school who speaks the language of the child, draw pictures to communicate with the child. Draw a clock with pictures of what happens during the day at certain times, such as children playing when it is time for recess, etc.

4. *Physical Activity:* Make sure that all ESL students are heavily involved during those times in the school day when physical exercise is taken. Never remove them from PE or recess, even for extra language study. Physical activity can serve to mitigate the effects of stress, is an optimum time for new ESL students to compete on even terms with their peers (thus restoring self-worth), can be an excellent chance for students to bond with their peers, and is an opportunity for "informal" language learning to take place.

5. *Welcome Ceremony:* Set aside some time for the new child to meet his/her classmates. Have a group of students act as a welcoming committee and plan a mini-party in which food and small gifts are shared with the newcomer to make him/her feel as if he/she were a valued addition to the group. Introduce the child to the class and have each student introduce him or herself to the newcomer and greet him/her with a warm "Welcome!"

6. *Community Orientation:* Arrange for a student or group of students to take the newcomer on a tour of the community. A visit to the local market, if in a traditional culture community, would be an excellent place to begin as markets are often intimidating, yet are the centers of life in many areas. Have the students show the child what things are available, how the system of economic transactions functions (i.e., bargaining, etc.), and how to get around in the community.

7. *Parent Involvement:* Make sure that the parents of the new child are thoroughly oriented to the policies and routines of the school so that the child may use them as a resource after the school day is over.

Multicultural Stories

Prevention:	Security, Control, Self-worth
Curricular Areas:	All Curricular Areas
Grades:	2-5
Size:	Individual, small group or full class
Time:	30-45 minutes
Purpose:	To help students recognize their positive qualities and the trusted adults who are available to help them with life decisions.
Outcomes:	*The students will be able to:* 1. Identify some of their talents, skills, interests and abilities; 2. Create a picture of a job or vocation they hope to have some day; 3. Name the trusted adults who care about them; 4. Find stories of real-life heroes who show courage or bravery.
Materials:	1. Drawing paper 2. Paints or markers 3. Newspapers or magazines 4. Glue 5. Scissors 6. Outline of a shield
Procedures:	Read each of the following children's books and follow up with the specific activity:

a. Book: *Crow Boy* by Taro Yashima

On the first day of classes, Chibi, a small, shy Japanese boy hides beneath the building because he is afraid of the teacher and other children. He becomes a loner, and other classmates tease him. The teacher gets to know Chibi and discovers many of his hidden talents. By sharing his talent of crow imitations at the end-of-the-year talent show, Chibi gains respect and acceptance.

Activity: Discuss how the teacher in *Crow Boy* showed she cared about him. Ask students to name other adults who care about them. Fold an 8" x 11" paper in half twice to create four sections. Direct students to draw a picture of a trusted adult who cares about them in each section. Allow time to share their pictures of trusted adults with other students.

b. Book: *The Legend of Indian Paintbrush* by Tomie dePaola

Little Gopher is the smallest Indian boy in his tribe and is unable to keep up with the other boys who are learning to become warriors. The shaman of the tribe tells him that he has another talent, and his people will remember him honorably for his talent. Little Gopher follows his Dream Vision and becomes great among his people through painting pictures for his tribe on buckskin.

Activity: Discuss how Little Gopher's talent, dream and the shaman's encouragement helped him find his life's work. Give the students a piece of drawing paper and paints or markers. Direct them to think about their talents and draw a picture of what they are hoping to be when they grow up. Allow time for students to share their dream vision with other students.

c. **Book:** *Amazing Grace* by Mary Hoffman

Grace is a girl with an amazing imagination who believes in herself and is confident that she can do anything. She begins to doubt herself when her classmates point out that she cannot play the part in the classroom production of *Peter Pan* because she is black and a girl. Grace is inspired to practice for the part in the class play after her grandmother takes her to see the ballet, *Romeo and Juliet*, where a black ballerina dances the lead role. Her hard work practicing for the part pays off when the class unanimously selects her to be Peter Pan.

Activity: Discuss Grace's talent (imagination), skill (dancing), interest (being in a play), and positive quality (hard-working). Give the students an outline of a shield divided into four sections. Direct them to draw a picture of one of their talents, skills, interests and positive qualities in each section. Allow time for the students to share their shield with the other students.

d. **Book:** *Nessa's Fish* by Nancy Luen

Nessa is an Inuit girl who walks a great distance with her grandmother to find a good salmon fishing area. When the grandmother becomes ill, Nessa must protect her grandmother and their fish from a fox, wolf and bear. She shows herself to be quick-witted and brave. Nessa's family is proud of her when they eventually arrive to help her grandmother and Nessa home.

Activity: Discuss the meaning of courage or bravery and how Nessa acted in a brave way. Direct the students to find an example of a person in the newspaper or a magazine who acted in a courageous way. Allow time for the students to share their story with the group.

Overcoming Difficulties by Linda Burrell Hill, 1994, Teacher Created Materials, Inc., Huntington Beach, CA, is filled with activities in all curricular areas to expand on these four stories.

Reducing Test Stress

Prevention: Self-worth, Security, Control

Curricular Areas: Any area

Grades: 2-6

Size: Full class

Time: 60 minutes

Purpose: To help reduce students' anxiety about taking standardized tests and build their confidence in developing test-taking strategies to assist them.

Outcomes: *The students will be able to:*
1. Identify ways to prepare themselves for taking a test;
2. Role play and practice some test-taking strategies to use during a test;
3. Take tests with less anxiety.

Materials: 1. Teacher-made sample tests
2. Paper
3. #2 Pencils

Procedures: 1. Preparing ahead of time to do well on a test includes eating a good breakfast or healthy food, getting a good night's rest, practicing relaxation exercises and bringing materials needed for the test to school.
2. Students can make their own simple graph chart to keep records or check off each way to prepare for a test.
3. Students will feel more secure about taking a test if they practice test-taking strategies that put them in control of the testing situation.
4. Teach the following strategies. Use role-playing of each strategy as well as actual practice on teacher-made practice tests to reinforce learning of strategies.
    a. Listen to or read test directions carefully. (The teacher can read directions for the students to follow and provide written directions to read and follow.)
    b. Make your best guess. Cross out and eliminate answers you know are wrong and look for any clues in the remaining answers to help you decide.
    c. If the test must be completed in a certain amount of time, work at a medium pace and do not spend too much time on one question. Be sure to allow time to answer questions you know.
    d. If time allows, be sure to double-check your answers to make sure nothing is left out.
    e. Breathe slowly and remain calm throughout the test.
5. The more practice the students experience, the easier it will be for them to use the strategies in a test-taking situation.

Architects

Prevention: Control, Security, Self-worth

Curricular Areas: Language Arts, Science, Art, Social Studies

Grades: 2-8

Size: Full class

Time: 30 minutes

Purpose: To help the students experience working together and communicating with others non-verbally

Outcomes: *The students will be able to:*
1. Construct a structure using straws or tinker toys within a time limit;
2. Work and cooperate with others in small groups;
3. Communicate non-verbally with other group members;
4. Evaluate their ability to perform outcomes 1, 2 and 3 above.

Materials: Tinker toys or straws and tape

Procedures:
1. Divide the students into groups of no more than five or six students. Give each group the same amount of tinker toys or straws and tape. Explain to them that they have 15 minutes to build a structure together. They may not speak to each other, but they may communicate nonverbally.
2. You can give each group a total number of points for following directions, completing a structure and communicating nonverbally while subtracting points for verbal communication. Explain this carefully before you begin.
3. When the time limit is up, allow time to evaluate the activity. Discuss the following:
   a. How they communicated nonverbally;
   b. If people worked separately or together;
   c. How they feel about their structure;
   d. Behaviors that get in the way of group cooperation;
   e. How they worked within the group;
   f. What contributes to successful team work.

Balloon Esteem

Prevention:	Self-worth
Curricular Areas:	Language Arts
Grades:	2-8
Size:	Full class or small group
Time:	50 minutes

Purpose: To help children identify some of the outside influences which contribute to low self-esteem and some of their inner strengths that can build self-esteem.

Outcomes: *The students will be able to:*
1. Identify the outside factors that contribute to low self-esteem;
2. Identify their strengths that contribute to high self-esteem;
3. Learn coping skills when struggling with low self-esteem;
4. Hear ways that other children cope with low self-esteem.

Materials:
1. Two balloons per student
2. Permanent markers

Procedures:
1. Allow students to blow up their balloons and write down all of the outside factors that make them feel bad about themselves or that contribute to low self-esteem.
2. Have students discuss these outside factors and influences.
3. Instruct students to pop the balloons that contain the factors for low self-esteem.
4. Allow students to blow up the second balloons and write or draw a picture of all their strengths and things that make them feel good about themselves or that contribute to high self-esteem.
5. Discuss the activity with the students having them focus on the following:
   a. What types of things make them feel good about themselves?
   b. How do they cope when they feel badly about themselves?
   c. What can they do to prevent outside factors from lowering their selfesteem?

Feeling Masks

Prevention:	Security, Control
Curricular Areas:	Art, Social Studies, Language Arts
Grades:	3-5
Size:	Full class
Time:	60-180 minutes
Purpose:	To help students realize that we have many different feelings and recognize how we communicate our feelings to others.
Outcomes:	*The students will be able to:* 1. Listen to a poem and identify feeling words; 2. Name a variety of feelings people have; 3. Create a feeling mask; 4. Identify what causes feelings and role play how we act when we feel different ways.
Materials:	1. The poem, "I Have Feelings." 2. Materials for masks: See the following page.
Procedures:	1. This activity can be carried out as simply or as involved as the teacher may choose. The main idea is to make feeling masks using paper plates, paper bags or paper mache. 2. Read the poem, "I Have Feelings" to the students. Ask the students to listen for feelings that are mentioned in the poem:

I Have Feelings

I have feelings, and you do too,
I'd like to share a few with you.
Sometimes I'm happy, and sometimes I'm sad,
Sometimes I'm scared, and sometimes I'm mad.
The most important feeling, you see,
Is that I'm proud of being me.

> No one sees the things I see;
> Behind my eyes is only me.
> And no one knows where my feelings begin,
> For there's only me inside my skin.
> No one knows what I can do;
> I'll be me, and you be you.

>> It's a wonderful thing how everyone owns,
>> Just enough skin to cover his bones.
>> My dad's would be too big to fit;
>> I'd be all wrinkled inside of it.
>> Baby sister's would be much too small;
>> It wouldn't cover me up at all.
>> I feel just right in the skin I wear—
>> There's no one like me anywhere.

3. As the students name the feelings they heard or any other feelings people have, write them on a board or chart. Some feeling words that will work well with the mask-making activity are the following:

happy	*sad*	*angry*
excited	*afraid*	*brave*
proud		

4. Explain to the student they will be making masks that show these feelings. The type of masks being made will determine the demonstration. The masks can be made individually or in small groups.
5. When the masks are completed, use them with the students in a large group or in small groups to identify the time when we have these feelings and act out with the mask what we do when we feel angry, sad, happy, etc.
6. The mask can be used throughout the year and can also decorate an area of the classroom.

Masks and Materials

A. Paper Plate Masks
     Paper plates
     Scissors
     Markers or crayons
     Flat wooden sticks or string

Cut eyes in the plates and use markers or crayons to draw the facial expressions. A stick can be glued to the plate at the bottom to hold the plate to one's face or string can be attached at each side to tie it on.

B. Paper Bag Masks
     Paper bags (brown or white)
     Scissors
     Markers, crayons or paints

Cut eyes in the bags and use markers, crayons or paints to create the face.

C. Paper Mache Masks
     Paper (newspaper or newsprint)
     Flour and water paste or glue
     Balloons or some other curved form
     Tempera paint
     Brushes
     Shellac or clear varnish

Tear paper into strips and dip in a flour paste mixture or glue-water mixture (thin, creamy consistency) for a minute or two until soaked. Layer the wet strips over half an inflated balloon or other curved form and build up to a one-quarter inch thickness. Let dry completely. Trim edges, cut opening for eyes and use tempera paints to create the facial expression. The masks can be coated with a shellac or clear varnish to preserve them.

Families at Work

Prevention:	Control, Security
Curricular Areas:	Social Studies, Language Arts
Grades:	3-5
Size:	Full class
Time:	30-40 minutes per visit
Purpose:	To help the students realize that families work together to support each other and help them learn to become independent adults.
Outcomes:	*The students will be able to:*

1. Identify how the jobs and careers of family members contribute to the family;
2. Name some rewards that a family experiences because of the work family members perform;
3. Identify ways that their work contribute to the good of the family;
4. Recognize similarities and differences in the work their families perform.

Materials: None

Procedures:

1. Schedule time throughout the year for each child to invite one or more members of his/her family to visit the classroom to talk about their career or work. A suggestion is to send a letter home at the beginning of the year explaining this project.
2. Before the first visit, have the students find some information in the library or elsewhere on various jobs/careers. Ask them to think about questions they may want to ask the visitor about his/her job, such as the following:
    a. What is your training?
    b. What are your hours?
    c. What are your responsibilities?
    d. What do you like and not like about your work?
    e. What kind of special equipment do you use?
3. Encourage the visitors to bring any special equipment, tools or other items representative of their work. Discuss with the class and visitor(s) how the work they do outside the home contributes to the family. What fun things can the family enjoy because of the jobs that family members have?
4. As a follow-up to any visit, have the children write their own resume listing jobs and work that they perform. Discuss how their work contributes to the family.

But I Can...

Prevention:	Self-worth
Curricular Areas:	Language Arts, Social Studies
Grades:	3-5
Size:	Full class
Time:	45 minutes
Purpose:	To help children overcome difficult situations through realizing their potential and worth, regardless of skill or knowledge base.

Outcomes:

The students will be able to:
1. Identify situations where they feel unworthy or not up to the challenge;
2. Practice statements that increase self-worth regardless of ability or previous knowledge;
3. Discuss alternatives to feelings of worthlessness;
4. Generate options for use in other experiences.

Materials:

1. List of short statements (provided as a hand-out)
2. List of phrases for the facilitator to read

Procedures:

1. Place cut-out statements in a paper bag and ask all students to choose one at random.
2. Write the words **BUT I CAN...**on the blackboard.
3. Read the facilitator's phrases one at a time to the class. Ask the students to stand up if their statement can apply to the situation. Go around the room and have the students read their statements aloud to the class, adding BUT I CAN...to the front of the statement.
     Example:　Phrase – "I am always picked last..."
     Student – "BUT I CAN work hard for my team."
4. Check if any other students have a phrase that will work after all students that are standing have read their statements and discuss those responses.
5. Continue reading phrases as long as time allows and be sure to add your own phrases based upon your knowledge of the class and what situations are bothering them.
6. Discuss the responses and how thinking in a negative way about themselves can be changed and replaced with different options and attitudes.

* It is important to stress to students that they look at the situations in a different way than they may be doing. This will encourage more positive thinking among the group.

List of student statements:

TRY HARD FOR MY TEAM

BE A GOOD FRIEND TO OTHERS

HELP OTHERS WHEN NEEDED

LISTEN WHEN SOMEONE NEEDS ME

COMFORT SOMEONE WHEN NEEDED

WORK HARD

TRY MY BEST

BE THERE

ALWAYS BE KIND

BE HONEST

Facilitator's phrases:

I ALWAYS GET PICKED LAST…

I'M NOT THE MOST POPULAR…

I'M NOT THE BEST PLAYER…

I DON'T ALWAYS MAKE GREAT CHOICES…

I'M NOT THE SMARTEST IN THE CLASS…

AMIGO

Prevention:	Security
Curricular Areas:	Language Arts
Grades:	3-6
Size:	Small group or full class
Time:	60 minutes
Purpose:	To help students recognize the qualities needed to be a friend.

Outcomes:

The students will be able to:
1. Discuss the importance of friendships;
2. List the qualities needed to be a friend;
3. Identify the friendship qualities they possess;
4. Identify the qualities they want to develop in order to be a better friend.

Materials:

1. AMIGO cards – tag board cards or paper with 5 vertical and 5 horizontal lines creating 25 squares with the letters A-M-I-G-O at the top of each column
2. Objects or paper to cover the squares

Procedures:

1. Discuss and list the reasons why friends are important.
2. Identify and list 25 or more qualities of a friend (i.e., A friend is someone who is…patient, kind, caring, respectful, dependable, trustworthy, helpful, honest, truthful, thoughtful, loyal, faithful, just, understanding, accepting, fair, encouraging, mannerly, nice, responsible, fun, interesting, cooperative, courteous, considerate, generous, cheerful, agreeable, affectionate, sincere, reliable).
3. Explain how "amigo" is the word for "friend" in Spanish. Have each student randomly fill in each square on the AMIGO card with a friendship quality.
4. Play the AMIGO game by calling out a friendship quality as it is pulled from a container. Play until a diagonal, vertical or horizontal line is covered.
5. Ask the students to circle the friendship qualities they have on their cards.
6. Direct students to star the friendship qualities they want to develop on their cards. Discuss how they can develop these qualities.

Drawing on My Emotions

Prevention:	Security, Control
Curricular Areas:	Art, Language Arts
Grades:	3-6
Size:	Full class
Time:	40 minutes
Purpose:	To help student identify and communicate fears.
Outcomes:	*The students will be able to:* 1. Express feelings; 2. Communicate feelings; 3. Identify and talk about fears.
Materials:	1. Paints 2. Crayons 3. Paper
Procedures:	1. Introduce activity to the class and ask members to create drawings of what makes them feel happy, sad, mad, scared or surprised. 2. Discuss situations where the child has felt these feelings. 3. Discuss what would help the situations that were fearful such as having a friend nearby or having someone to talk to.

Goals Versus Expectations

Prevention: Self-worth, Control

Curricular Areas: Physical Education

Grades: 3-8

Size: Small group

Time: 30 minutes

Purpose: To help individuals realize the emotional effects of irrational expectations and how to set realistic goals that will help them to be successful.

Outcomes: *The students will be able to:*
1. Demonstrate the ability to base their success on meeting realistic goals and not irrational expectations;
2. Negotiate their goals based upon current abilities.

Materials:
1. Basketball hoop
2. Basketball

Procedures:
1. Encourage students to simply shoot the basketball.
2. Increase challenges to the activity such as range and type of shot.
3. Try to create a small degree of frustration based upon their inability to make shots outside a certain range.
4. Encourage students to make five shots in a row from a difficult place.
5. Once it seems that the point of frustration has been reached, encourage the participant to set a realistic goal to make a certain amount of shots in a certain period of time.
6. Discuss how it feels to either meet or not meet this goal in comparison to the other goal.
7. Compare the two differing emotional states experienced between meeting goals and trying to live up to expectations.
8. Discuss other aspects of goal-setting, including how to use "step-wise" smaller goals to meet larger goals. This should include the possibility of increasing or decreasing measures within a goal if they prove to be too difficult or not challenging enough.
9. Variations of this exercise can be with many activities so use your imagination.

My Song

Prevention:	Self-worth, Security, Control
Curricular Areas:	Social Studies, Art, History, Language Arts
Grades:	3-8
Size:	Full class
Time:	60 minutes
Purpose:	To help students express and release emotions while also identifying alternate ways to express emotions.
Outcomes:	*The students will be able to:* 1. Express emotions through different forms of communication; 2. Express his or her current emotional status.
Materials:	1. CD player or tape player 2. Several musical selections (preferably without lyrics)
Procedures:	1. Have students listen to music selections. 2. Have students pick a song or musical piece that helps them express their current feelings. 3. Ask the students to write down what feelings they experience during the playing of the various songs. 4. Ask the students to share with the class their choice of music and what feelings they feel are expressed in the music.

My Stellar Self

Prevention: Self-worth, Security, Control

Curricular Areas: Social Studies, Language Arts, Art

Grades: 4-8

Size: Full class

Time: 40 minutes

Purpose: To help students identify personal characteristics they possess and those they wish to develop.

Outcomes: *The students will be able to:*
1. Identify their attributes;
2. Communicate their attributes;
3. Identify what attributes they would like to possess;
4. Create strategies to develop desired attributes.

Materials: 1. White paper
2. Colored pencils
3. Star stickers

Procedures: 1. Ask the class to list the attributes that they possess or would like to possess on a sheet of paper entitled " My Stellar Self." Mark those they would like to have with a star next to the word.
2. Ask members of the class to share their list and consult with other classmates about how to develop the characteristics that they would like to possess.

Senoian Dream Work

Prevention:	Control, Security
Curricular Areas:	Creative Writing, Social Studies, Geography, Art, Drama
Grades:	4-8
Size:	Groups
Time:	45 minutes
Purpose:	To help students deal with their fears through creative expression.

Outcomes:

The students will be able to:
1. Recall and relate their dreams to their peers;
2. Create art, stories or plays based on materials from their dreams;
3. Gain support from their peers in dealing with fears expressed in dreams;
4. Cope better with the fears expressed in their dreams.

Materials:

1. Drawing paper
2. Colored pencils
3. Pens
4. Paints
5. Writing paper

Procedures:

1. Dreams can be used educationally as material for creative writing, drama and art projects while at the same time providing catharsis for the fears that emerge during our sleeping hours. The following instructions can be read to the class as a beginning to a set of creative activities dealing with dreams:

"Dreams are important because they give us access to material that is not available while we are awake. At night, when our defenses are down, our emotions express themselves freely and in strange ways. Negative emotions, such as fear, anger and hostility, often leave the greatest impression on us as nightmares. However, the dream world is also a place where positive emotions express themselves, and if we can find ways of understanding this information, it can enrich our waking hours.

The Senoi [rhymes with annoy] are a people who live in the Central Malay Peninsula. They believe that dreams are very important, and they are taught from a very young age how to work with their dreams. When they wake up after a dream, they often try to continue the dream in their imagination, talk to some of the characters in their dreams and finish what was left unfinished. If they dream of falling, for example, they imagine that they are falling to some place and that they land safely, and they look around to see what they can learn from this place. If they dream that a frightening stranger chases them, they turn around in their imagination and confront the stranger in order to ask the person what he or she wants or what he or she is trying to tell them.

Now I'd like for all of you to get into groups of about three or four, and if you're comfortable talking about some of your dreams, see what you can remember, and perhaps some of you have had some of the same experiences in your dreams. Ask yourselves how the dreams made you feel? Perhaps you will want to go in your imagination back to a dream and talk with someone in the dream or continue the dream and see where it leads."

2. As extensions of this exercise, have students do some of the following:
    a. Write a short story using their dream as the starting point;
    b. Draw a picture or a story board of a dream and its resolution;
    c. Make a group painting of a dream;
    d. Make up a skit or short play around one of the group member's dreams.

Source: Clower, G. A pilot counseling project for preadolescent girls. Unpublished paper.

Win, Lose, Draw

Prevention:	Security
Curricular Areas:	Any Curricular Area
Grades:	4-8
Size:	Full class, groups
Time:	30-40 minutes
Purpose:	To help the students experience working together as a group.

Outcomes:

The students will be able to:
1. Communicate with each other verbally and non-verbally to identify a word or phrase;
2. Evaluate what behaviors are needed to work cooperatively in a group.

Materials:

1. Vocabulary words or phrases from any content area written on small pieces of paper
2. Chalk board and chalk or flip chart and marker
3. Clock with second hand or other type of timer

Procedures:

1. This game is similar to charades or Pictionary. Divide the class into two teams. Explain to the students that one team member at a time is given a paper with a word or phrase written on it. The team member draws symbols or pictures to give the other members of the team clues about the word. Letters of the alphabet or numbers may not be a part of the drawings, but parts of the word may be written on the board or chart as they are guessed. The person drawing may not speak, but other team members may call out their guesses as they think of them.
2. The time limit is usually 3 minutes, but this may be adjusted to the group. If the team guesses the word or phrase within the time limit, they will receive a point. If not, the other team may make one guess and if correct, they receive a point. Play is alternated between the two teams.
3. After each team has had an equal number of turns, discuss what helped each team to successfully guess the words or phrases. What hindered them?

This is a good game for introducing or reinforcing vocabulary words.

Cooperative Outdoor Games

Prevention: Security, Control, Self-worth

Curricular Areas: Physical Education, Social Studies, Language Arts

Grades: 4-8

Size: Full class or small group

Time: 5-10 minutes per activity

Purpose: To help students improve their communication and problem-solving skills through participation in cooperative games.

Outcomes: *The students will be able to:*
1. Cooperate with other students in small groups to complete a task;
2. Communicate verbally and non-verbally with other students in a small group;
3. Assess a problem, generate possible solutions in a small group and participate in making a group decision;
4. Offer support and encouragement to each other in a small group to complete a task.

Materials:
1. Balls (kick ball size)
2. Small platform or sturdy table

Procedures: The following activities generally require a large open space. Exercise caution to limit the risk of injury during these activities. Describe the nature of the activity to be attempted and provide a demonstration when appropriate. One suggestion for grouping students into smaller groups or pairs is by birthday months.

1. *Lap Ball:* All players sit in a very close circle, shoulder to shoulder, legs stretched and straight out in front. The object of the game is to pass the ball from lap to lap around the circle X number of times without using hands. A large group could be divided into two groups to see which group can pass it most quickly.

2. *Pass and Catch:* Have the players line up in two parallel lines, each facing another person, about 10 feet (3 meters) apart. The first person in one line throws the ball to the person directly opposite him or her, then runs to the end of his/her respective line, and the next person quickly moves up. Repeat the entire line as many times as desired.

3. *All Aboard:* This requires a small platform or sturdy table not quite big enough to accommodate the group. Ask all members to get on the platform and stay on it for 5 seconds.

4. *Stand Up:* With a partner, players sit back to back, arms interlocked at the elbows with knees bent. The object is to stand up. A variation of this activity is to try it with 3, 4 or 5 players.

5. *Python Pentathlon:* All group members are seated on the floor in a line, and each student puts his or her legs around the waist of the person in front. The group is then instructed to move to a pre-determined point.

6. ***Knots:*** All players stand in a circle, shoulder to shoulder, and then grasp hands, one with each hand. Players are not to grasp the hands of the persons next to them. Then, untie the knot without anyone letting go of the hands that he/she holds. Pivoting the hands without breaking the grasp is permissible.

7. ***Four Pointers:*** The object is to get the group to move from Point A to Point B with only six supporting points (feet, arms or knees) touching the ground. Distance to be traveled, number of supporting points and number in each group can be varied depending on the skill level of the group.

Source: Duncan, K., Beck, D. L., & Granum, R. A. (1988). Project explore: An acitivity-based counseling group. The School Counselor, 35(3), 215-219.

Perception

Prevention:	Self-worth
Curricular Areas:	Language Arts
Grades:	4-8
Size:	Full class or small group
Time:	30 minutes
Purpose:	To help students realize that even though things appear to be the same that perception is not always a reality.
Outcomes:	*The students will be able to:*

1. Identify negative characteristics in relation to an object;
2. Identify positive characteristics in relation to an object;
3. Discuss ways in which characteristics are perceived and how perception changes how people view each other, especially those who are different than themselves.

Materials: Bag of marbles (all the same)

Procedures:

1. Ask students to choose one marble from the bag.
2. Have each student say one negative thing about another person's marble then one positive thing about the same person's marble.
3. Continue through the group until all students have heard something about their marbles.
4. Discuss the statements made and how so many things can be said about things that are exactly the same.
5. Relate the discussion to people and how perception can be changed simply by the way someone is thought about or looked at.
6. Ask students how they felt about the negative statement made to them, especially since they knew their marble was exactly the same as the other person's marble.
7. Have students discuss the impact that a negative perception or statement can have on them and their feelings of self-worth.

* It is important for this exercise that all marbles be exactly the same. Some children may look for differences but assure them in the beginning that they all are alike.

Who Am I?

Prevention:	Self-worth
Curricular Areas:	Social Studies, Language Arts
Grades:	5-8
Size:	Full class
Time:	60 minutes
Purpose:	To help students identify and analyze their strengths, interests, goals and skills.

Outcomes:

The students will be able to:
1. Identify strengths, interests, goals and skills;
2. Share with other members of the class their personal successes, characteristics, goals and achievements.

Materials:

1. "Who Am I?" worksheet
2. Colored pencils, markers or crayons
3. Colored construction paper
4. Scissors
5. Magazines

Procedures:

1. Introduce activity and ask students to create their individual collages by expressing the answers on their worksheets (next page) in pictures.
2. When the students are finished creating their collages, allow time for each student to share one or two areas of their collages with the class.

Who Am I?

The most important thing about me is _____ .

I am good at _____ .

A secret ambition of mine is _____ .

A career goal of mine is to become a _____ .

A value that I hold as most important is _____ .

A person I most admire and want to be like is _____ .

If I had lots of money, I would _____ .

I like people who _____ .

20 Questions

Prevention: Self-worth, Security, Control

Curricular Areas: Social Studies, Language Arts

Grades: 5-8

Size: Full class

Time: 60 minutes

Purpose: To help students identify common interests in peers and to help foster relationship building.

Outcomes: *The students will be able to:*
1. Identify what they have in common with other individuals;
2. Express what differences exist between individuals;
3. Demonstrate skills in relationship building

Materials: 20 questions worksheet (next page)

Procedures:
1. Introduce activity to the class and ask members to pair off.
2. Have pairs ask each other the "20 Questions" worksheet.
3. Have pairs introduce each other using what information they gathered from the "20 Questions" worksheet.

20 Questions

1. What is your name?

2. What do you like to do?

3. Why?

4. Where do you live?

5. What is your favorite food?

6. What is your favorite animal?

7. Why?

8. What kinds of sports do you play?

9. What kinds of sports do you wish you played?

10. What do you like to do on the weekends?

11. Why?

12. Do you want to go to college?

13. What do you want to be when you grow up?

14. Why?

15. What makes you angry?

16. What makes you happy?

17. What makes you sad?

18. What do you like best about school?

19. What do you like best about this group?

20. Why?

Family Album

Prevention: Self-worth, Security, Control

Curricular Areas: Social Studies, Art, History

Grades: 5-8

Size: Full class

Time: 60 minutes

Purpose: To establish and recognize a network of support within the family.

Outcomes: *The students will be able to:*
                         1. Identify those who can provide help when coping with fears.

Materials: 1. Photographs of family members, including family friends and extended
                            family
                         2. Construction paper
                         3. Tape or glue

Procedures: 1. Have students select pictures of their family and friends.
                         2. Have students assemble and tape or glue pictures into a collage onto the construction
                            paper.
                         3. Ask the students to share with the class who is in the pictures and how these people can
                            help with easing their fears.

Oral History Project

Prevention:	Self-worth, Control, Security
Curricular Areas:	Social Studies, Language Arts
Grades:	5-8
Size:	Individual, small group or full class
Time:	3-4 class periods
Purpose:	To help students recognize life-coping skills through the experiences of a person of an older generation.

Outcomes:

The students will be able to:
1. Interview an older adult about his/her life experiences;
2. Develop and write a story about the older adult's life from their interview notes;
3. Share their story with others;
4. Discuss the life-coping skills of the person interviewed.

Materials: Computer

Procedures:

1. Invite persons born in the first half of the 20th century to participate in an oral history project (grandparents, senior citizens from the community, residents of a retirement home).
2. Help the students identify historical events from the first half of the 20th century.
3. Create a list of interview questions with the students. Focus on questions in the following categories: challenging situations, difficult decisions, historical events, worries, accomplishments, successes, ways of coping, etc.
4. Match students with an older adult to conduct their interview.
5. Guide students to develop a story of the older adult's life from their interview information. Create a final draft in the computer lab.
6. Plan a gathering of the older adults with refreshments where the students can read their stories. The students may share a copy of their finished story with the older adult.
7. Follow up the project with a discussion of life-coping skills. What were the difficult or challenging life experiences of the person you interviewed? How did they cope with these experiences? Who helps them in difficult situations? What did they learn from this project?

PACE

Prevention:	Control, Security, Self-worth
Curricular Areas:	Social Studies, Language Arts
Grades:	6-8
Size:	Full class or groups
Time:	60-180 minutes, several class periods
Purpose:	To help the students realize that evaluating alternatives and their consequences is helpful in making decisions and solving problems.

Outcomes:

The students will be able to:

1. List decisions they have made during the previous day and identify the consequences of those decisions;
2. Identify problems that students their age have;
3. Name the steps of the PACE model;
4. Explain the steps of the PACE model;
5. Illustrate the use of the steps of the PACE model through role-playing a problem situation;
6. Create their own decision-making model and teach it to other students.

Materials: None

Procedures:

1. Ask the students to write down at least 10 decisions (no matter how small) they have made in the last day (24 hours). Ask them also to record the consequences of their decisions and whether the consequences were negative or positive for them.

For example:

Decisions	Consequences	- or +
a. Selected clothes for school	were uncomfortable	-
	received compliments	+
b.Watched TV instead of studying for a test	flunked the test	-
	enjoyed the show	+

2. Discuss how decisions sometimes have negative and positive consequences. When we weigh the negative and positive consequences ahead of time, we can make a better choice.
3. Now ask the students to list 10 problems that they feel students their age have to cope with. They may be school-, friend- or home-related problems.

4. Teach the steps of the PACE decision-making model:

    P   **Problem**   Identify the problem specifically

    A   **Alternatives**   Explore all the possible alternatives and the
                                           consequences of each

    C   **Choose** a plan of action   Decide on one of the alternatives

    E   **Evaluate** the results   Was it a good decision? Why or why
            of your decision   not?

5. Break into small groups (4-5) and, using a problem that the students
    identify, apply the model and ask them to prepare a role play (skit showing
    the steps of the model being used to make a decision).

6. After the skit presentations, discuss how effective or helpful the model was in making
    decisions. An excellent follow-up is to give students time in small groups to design their
    own decision-making model and to teach it to the class in a creative way. They must be
    sure to include the basic steps of any decision-making model. If equipment is available,
    videotaping them teaching their model is very effective.

Planning a *Real* School Project

Prevention: Control, Security, Self-worth

Curricular Areas: Any Curricular Area

Grades: 6-8

Size: Full class

Time: May be accomplished over several months

Purpose: To help the students experience making decisions, working with peers and
                       contributing to the school through planning a service project.

Outcomes: *The students will be able to:*
                       1. Generate ideas for service projects;
                       2. Make a group decision selecting a project;
                       3. Plan the necessary steps to accomplish the project;
                       4. Implement the steps to the completion of the project.

Materials: None

Procedures:
1. Present the idea of undertaking a class project that will benefit the school and
   other students and make a lasting, tangible contribution to the school.
   Explain that this will be an opportunity to work together as a group, make
   decisions and feel a sense of accomplishment.
2. The students should generate their own ideas, select one project as a group, plan the
   timeline and steps, identify materials and resources, decide tasks and assign
   responsibilities.
3. Time will have to be set aside weekly for planning, and the project selected will need the
   administration's approval. Some projects that other schools have implemented include the
   following:
   a. Building an obstacle course
   b. Creating and performing a puppet show
   c. Raising money to purchase new library books
   d. Planting and harvesting a garden
   e. Painting a mural in the school
   f. Improving the landscaping of the campus
4. Be sure to allow time for evaluation during and at the completion of the projects. It will
   be helpful for students to access the following:
   a. How they feel about the project
   b. How the group is cooperating
   c. How students are cooperating within the group
   d. What they have learned about themselves and others

Web Sites

The following Web sites may be helpful in understanding childhood fears and anxiety disorders. They may be used to collect further information for the reader or as resources for parents and others.

http://www.shpm.com
     Self-help & Psychology Magazine

http://www.ucalgary.ca/~dkbrown/index
     The Children's Literature Web Guide

http://www.hhpl.on.ca/libraryhhpl/childrens/resour
     Other sites of interest to parents, caregivers and educators

http://www.child.net/ycnews
     Youth and Children News

http://www.maginationpress.com
     Magination Press – Books for Children's Special Needs

http://www.indiana.edu/~eric_rec/ieo/digests
     Using Literature to Help Children Cope With Problems

http://trfn.clh.org/pcgc/fears
     Children's Fears Parent and Child Guidance Center of Pittsburgh

http://www.washburn.org
     Child Guidance

http://www.specialchild.com
     Children with Special Needs

http://www.agsnet.com
     American Guidance Services Prevention Books and Materials

http://ericcass.uncg.edu
     ERIC/CASS Prevention Books and Materials

http://www.educationalmedia.com/home.html-ssi
     Educational Media

Section 4

Appendices

Appendix I-A: Helping the Fearful Child – A Counseling Model

Introduction

The counseling model in this section is offered for those individuals who will engage in counseling activities with the individual or groups of individuals who are exhibiting the effects of dysfunction as a result of anxiety-related disorders. In addition to the model listed, recent findings suggest that family work can also be an appropriate intervention with the debilitating effects of children's fears. It is often times difficult for the school counselor, school psychologist or teacher to work with those interventions but a referral can sometimes be in the best interest of children who are experiencing difficulties. When making a referral, be sure to give the family several options and ask permission to follow up to make certain that the child and family are receiving appropriate care. When this is not possible, the following on family treatments for children's fears may be helpful. Another level of intervention is helping the child who is already experiencing fear-related problems. The longer fear-related problems persist, the more difficult it is to help the person find ways to overcome his/her fear.

In the following pages, we have outlined a four-phase counseling scheme that follows the model of coping (self-worth, control, security) suggested in this guide. In the first phase, the counselor is concerned with establishing a positive relationship, providing cathartic release, exploring the child's world and validating the child's fear. This last consideration is most important. The child's fears are real, no matter how mystical, imaginary or unthreatening they may appear to the observer.

The second phase deals with assessment. This does not necessarily mean testing, but rather getting to know the child from his or her perspective and developing a sense of how the child views the world and his/her place in it. Specifically, the counselor needs to have a clear picture of the child's sense of control, self-worth and security. It may be that a given fear arises out of a specific situation related to personal disaster in which the child feels vulnerable to a specific fear object. In such a situation, the counselor may move on to the third phase, focusing on the child's relationship with fear objects.

On the other hand, the counselor may find that the child's fears are many and varied arising from a lack of security. The child may have little opportunity to act on his/her world, seeing self at the mercy of things in the environment rather than exercising control over the environment. The child may view self as failure-expectant, assuming defeat in the face of life's threats. In such situations, the counselor will proceed into phase three with a different approach.

In phase three, the counselor is concerned with generating and implementing a plan of action to assist the child. For fear-specific situations, the counselor and child may implement a number of options, including systematic desensitization, implosive therapy, flooding, cognitive restructuring, cognitive self-control, bibliotherapy and relaxation training. Such strategies may be employed individually or in appropriate combination to help the child develop ways to cope with the fear object. If the fear object is a result of a lack of transference of the skills the child already has in coping, or as a result of a particular encounter, such specifically focused interventions have proven successful.

If the child's fears arise from a lack of control, self-worth and/or security, such approaches may help temporarily with the specific situation but will manifest themselves again in a different situation or with a different fear. In such cases, the counselor may proceed with some of the above strategies but will also want to help the child develop his/her general sense of control, self-worth and security.

Strategies the counselor may wish to employ here might include decision-making and problem-solving skills, increasing success experience, interpersonal communication skills training and assertiveness training. The counselor may work directly with the child in individual or group counseling but should also consider parent and teacher consultation. Consultation might focus on both helping parents and teachers understand childhood fear as well as home and classroom strategies to help the child develop a better sense of control, self-worth and security.

Evaluation

In the last phase, the counselor must assess the impact of the counseling strategies as helping the child deal with fear objects. If the counselor uses a direct strategy such as systematic desensitization, only to find that one fear object quickly replaces another fear object, the counselor may wish to look only at the child's sense of control, self-worth or security to determine if intervention in one or more areas underlying the child's sense of power would be an appropriate focus.

For children who have a positive sense of power, strategies focused on directly reducing the impact of the fear object may take a shorter period of time before results are noted than in the case where the child's sense of power is not strong. While intervention directed at the concepts of control, self-worth and security may take longer to show results, the long-term effects of helping children establish a sense of power in their lives will not only help with overcoming fear-related problems but may generalize to other areas of personal functioning.

Model for Counseling the Fearful Child

Stage One: Exploration

This stage allows the child to explore feelings, thoughts and behaviors openly regarding self in relation to fear object(s).

Counselor Seeks To:
- Establish an atmosphere of trust and open communication;
- Validate the child's perceptions as real and appropriate at the current level of experiencing and understanding;
- Provide an opportunity for catharsis.

Techniques Utilized:
- Empathic listening and responding
- Appropriate self-disclosure
- Biblio-Counseling
- Mutual storytelling
- Play and art therapy

Procedural Goal:
- Self-exploration

Stage Two: Assessment

This stage helps the child define the fear in relationship to trauma or disaster and/or current sense of security, self-worth and control.

Counselor Seeks To:
- Help the child recognize reactions to traumatic event or disaster;
- Help the child recognize sense of security, self-worth or control;
- Gently guide the child toward recognition of relationship of self with fear object.

Techniques Utilized:
- Continued empathic responding
- Added specificity in responding
- Role play
- Role reversal
- Play and art therapy
- Storytelling

Procedural Goal:
- Self-understanding

StageThree: Intervention

This stage helps the child take appropriate action to deal with fear object(s).

Counselor Seeks To:
- Help the child develop specific strategies in coping with fear object(s) and/or
- Help the child increase his/her sense of security and/or self-worth and/or control.

Techniques Utilized:
- Relaxation training
- Systematic desensitization
- Guided imagery
- Interpersonal communication skills training
- Decision making/problem-solving skills training
- Life skills training groups
- Creating success experiences
- Biblio-counseling
- Encouragement

Procedural Goal:
- Action directed toward dealing with fear object or increasing sense of security, self-worth and control

Stage Four: Evaluation

This stage helps the child assess current relationship of self to fear objects.

Counselor Seeks To:
- Validate child's ability to cope with fear object(s)
- Validate child's sense of security, self-worth and/or control.

Techniques Utilized:
- Role play
- Role rehearsal
- Role reversal
- Direct observation
- Indirect observation
- Self report

Procedural Goal:
- Evaluation of interaction scheme

Appendix I-B: Diagnostic Section

This section is meant to provide a quick reference for those who may have concerns that the issues and symptoms that children are experiencing have become excessively problematic in daily functioning such that they affect social, academic, or home functioning. Seven psychological disorders are listed below with common symptoms associated with these disorders as taken from the *Diagnostic and Statistical Manual IV – Text Revision* (APA, 2000).

Post-Traumatic Stress Disorder (PTSD)

Sometimes after a traumatic event some children will not develop any symptoms for several weeks or even months following the event. Parents and professionals should watch for symptoms that may indicate that the child has developed PTSD. Typical of these symptoms are the following:

1) Re-experiencing the event through dreams, flashbacks, or acting out the events in play
2) Being distant or feeling "emotionally numb"
3) Being overwhelmed emotionally by what was typically considered everyday situations and diminished interest in performing activities or pursuing typical interests
4) Crying spells or periods of uncontrolled crying
5) Isolating behaviors or avoiding family and friends
6) Poor concentration, irritability or regressive behaviors
7) Mood swings or feelings of anger or fear
8) Changes in sleep patterns, difficulty falling or staying asleep, sleeping too much and experiencing nightmares and/or sleep disturbances
9) Feelings of guilt about surviving the event or being unable to change the event or prevent the disaster
10) Feeling a sense of doom about the future
11) Routine avoidance of and reminders of the event
12) Being hypervigilant or having a startle reaction to common situations

Acute Stress Disorder

Acute Stress Disorder (ASD) is the development of characteristic anxiety, dissociative symptoms, and other symptoms that occur within 1 month after exposure to an extreme traumatic stressor. As a response to the traumatic event, the child develops intense fear, feelings of helplessness and/or horror. During or after the trauma and up to one month following, the child experiences a sense of numbing, detachment or a lack of emotional responsiveness. They may act as if in a daze, they may experience derealization or depersonalization and may have difficulty in recalling important aspects of the trauma. Other symptoms might include the following:

1) Persistent re-experiencing of the trauma through recurrent images, intrusive thoughts, dreams, or flashbacks
2) Avoidance of anything that reminds them of the trauma including avoidance of family,

friends, activities, places, etc.

3) Feelings of anxiety and increased arousal manifested in difficulty sleeping, irritability, poor concentration, hypervigilance, exaggerated startle response, or restlessness.

4) The child develops clinically significant distress or impairment in areas of functioning in social situations, activities or play and having difficulty performing normal tasks

5) Symptoms last for a period of at least two days and a maximum of 4 weeks following the crisis.

6) The symptoms are not a result of medication or substance use.

7) Children who develop at least three elements of dissociative symptoms (numbness, detachment, lack of emotional responsiveness, etc.), some fear of re-experiencing the trauma, avoidance behaviors and marked symptoms of anxiety for two days or more could have ASD. It is important to get appropriate mental health services to these children as soon as possible. ASD is a strong predictor of Post-Traumatic Stress Disorder (Birmes, Carreras, Ducasse, Charlet, Warner, Lauque, & Schmitt, 2001)

Specific Phobia (Phobic Anxiety Disorder)

Specific Phobia, formerly known as Simple Phobia, is characterized by a "persistent or recurrent fear (phobia) that is developmentally phase-appropriate (or was so at the time of onset) but which is abnormal in degree and is associated with significant social impairment" (WHO, 1994, p. 306). This is often difficult to detect in children because children and parents do not realize that fears are excessive or unreasonable and rarely report distress about having the phobia. This diagnosis is not made unless the fears lead to clinically significant impairment in social activities, social relationships, a person's normal routine, or academic functioning such as an unwillingness to go to school for fear of encountering a dog on the street (APA, 2000). The subtypes of specific phobias are listed below:

1) Animal Type-usually childhood onset
2) Natural Environment Type (i.e., storms, heights, or water) – usually childhood onset
3) Blood-injection-injury
4) Situational (i.e., public transportation, tunnels, bridges, elevators, flying, driving, enclosed places)
5) Other type (i.e., loud sounds, costumed characters)

Those who need to be assessed for specific phobias will display some of the following behaviors including a persistent fear that is excessive or unreasonable cued by the presence or anticipation of a specific object or situation such as those listed above in the subtypes. Children may display crying, tantrums, freezing, or clinging. Situations involving the specific object will be avoided or endured with extreme anxiety or distress.

Social Phobia (Social Anxiety Disorder)

Social phobia is characterized by an apprehension when encountering new, strange or socially threatening situations (WHO, 1994). It may include an interference in peer relationships due to fear of embarrassment or performance anxiety, so the activities designed for building support would aid in helping children to make peer connections and seek friends as allies. Young children may remain close to familiar adults, stay on the periphery of social activities, refuse to participate in group play, shrink from contact with others, and appear excessively timid in social settings (APA, 2000). Other symptoms in children include crying, tantrums, freezing, clinging or even mutism.

Generalized Anxiety Disorder (Overanxious Disorder of Childhood)

Generalized anxiety disorder is characterized by "extensive anxiety and worry" (WHO, 1994, p. 309). Children with this disorder may worry about the quality of their performance or competence at school or in sporting events, even when their performance is not being evaluated. In addition, they may worry about punctuality and catastrophic events. These children may be overly conforming, perfectionists, and unsure of themselves such that they redo tasks due to dissatisfaction or worry that it is not perfect. They are often overzealous in seeking approval and require excessive reassurance about their performance or other worries (APA, 2000). In children, these symptoms may present as any one of the following: restlessness, fatigue, difficulty concentrating, irritability, muscle tension, and sleep disturbance.

Separation Anxiety Disorder

Separation anxiety disorder is characterized by a developmentally inappropriate and "excessive anxiety concerning separation from home or from those to whom the person is attached" (APA, 1994, p. 110). Oftentimes, these children will express fear of being lost and never being reunited with their parents. They may be reluctant to attend school, camp, or sleepovers due to the separation from their parent(s). This anxiety concerning the separation may lead to social withdrawal, apathy, sadness, or difficulty concentrating. These children may not go to sleep without being near parents and may report having nightmares involving themes of separation. Physical symptoms may include headaches, stomachaches, nausea, or vomiting. These symptoms may occur in anticipation in addition to the actual separation from parents.

Panic Attacks, Panic Disorder, and Agoraphobia

Although not common in young children or young adolescents, panic attacks, agoraphobia, and panic disorder are types of anxiety-related disorders. Panic attacks include such symptoms as accelerated heart rate, sweating, trembling or shaking, shortness of breath, feelings of choking, chest pains, nausea, dizziness, fear of losing control, fear of dying, numbness or tingling, and chills or hot flashes. Panic disorder includes recurrent panic attacks and extreme worry about having additional attacks. Agoraphobia includes the fear of developing panic-like symptoms and being embarrassed due to these symptoms.

Adjustment Disorder

Adjustment disorder is a psychological response that develops within 3 months of exposure to an identifiable stressor or stressors, which results in clinically significant emotional or behavioral symptoms causing marked impairment in social or academic functioning. This diagnosis is only given if the stress-related disturbance does not meet the criteria for another specific Axis I disorder or is not an exacerbation of an Axis I or Axis II disorder. Adjustment disorder manifests in a number of different manners that include subtypes of adjustment disorder with depressed mood, anxiety, mixed anxiety and depressed mood, disturbance of conduct, and mixed disturbance of emotions and conduct.

Other Diagnostic Considerations

While this is a guideline and summary of the common disorders associated with excessive fear, stress, and trauma, this is not an exhaustive compendium of the disorders that may stem from fear, stress, and trauma. If concern exists for parents, teachers, or other professionals, it is best to refer the child to someone capable of assessing and making a diagnosis in order to cater treatment to the type of symptoms and disorder that the child is experiencing.

References

American Psychiatric Association. (2000). *Diagnostic and statistical manual of mental disorders* (4th ed., text revision). Washington, DC: Author.

Birmes, P., Carrerars, D., Ducasse, J., Charlet, J., Warner, B., Lauque, D., and Schmitt, L. (2001). Peritraumatic dissocation, acute stress, and early post traumatic stress disorder in victims of general crime. *Canadian Journal of Psychiatry, 46,* 649-651.

Kearney, C. A., & Wadiak, D. (1999). Anxiety disorders. In Netherton, S. D., Holmes, D., & Walker, C. E. (Eds.), Child and adolescent psychological disorders: A comprehensive textbook (pp. 282-303) New York: Oxford University Press.

World Health Organization (1994). *Pocket guide to the ICD-10 classification of mental and behavioral disorders*. Washington, DC: American Psychiatric Press.

Web Resources

http://www.surgeongeneral.gov/library/mentalhealth/chapter4/sec21.html#treatment
    Anxiety Disorders
http://helping.apa.org/therapy/anxiety.html
    APA Page on Anxiety Disorders

http://www.npi.ucla.edu/caap/
    Child and Adolescent Anxiety – UCLA

http://www2.mc.duke.edu/pcaad/
    Anxiety Disorders in Children – Duke University

http://www2.hawaii.edu/~chorpita/casap.html
    Child Anxiety – University of Hawaii

http://wwwaboutourkids.org/articles/med_anxiety.htm
    Anxiety Disorders in Children and Adolescents – New York University Child Study Center

Appendix I-C: Bibliography of Books About Children's Fears

Fear of Change

Coates, Belle. *Mak.* Houghton Mifflin, 1991. Ages 12 and up.
> In this slowly unfolding, well-written story of an orphaned boy torn between two cultures, the reader gains considerable insight into the feelings, beliefs and way of life of Native Americans, and in particular, their struggles to retain their culture. Change, Mak finds, is essential, yet change often pits the old ways against the new.

Fear of the Dark

Bond, Felicia. *Poinsettia Pig and the Firefighters.* Crowell Publishers, 1984. Ages 4-7.
> Lonely and afraid of the dark in her new room, Poinsettia Pig is comforted when she discovers that the firefighters are awake and keep watch during the night.

Bonsall, Crosby Newell. *Who's Afraid of the Dark?* Harper & Row, 1980. Ages 3-7.
> A little boy describes his dog's fear of the dark and his sympathetic friend, recognizing that it is the boy himself who is afraid, gives helpful advice.

Mayer, Mercer. *There's a Nightmare in My Closet.* Dial Press, 1968. Ages 3-6.
> In an amusing story, a determined young boy decides to take action against his nighttime fears.

Robinson, Deborah. *No Elephants Allowed.* Clarion Books, 1981. Ages 3-6.
> After receiving well-meant but ineffective help from his family, a little boy deals successfully and in his own way with his nighttime fears.

Schubert, Ingrid and Dieter. *There's a Crocodile Under My Bed.* McGraw Hill, 1981. Ages 3-6.
> A little girl copes with her bedtime fears by turning the frightening crocodile of her imagination into a gentle, entertaining fantasy, spending an evening with a delightful crocodile whose very job is to reassure her.

Smith, Janice Lee. *The Monster in the Third Dresser Drawer and Other Stories About Adam Joshua.* Harper & Row, 1981. Ages 5-8.
> In these anecdotal chapters, young Adam Joshua, with the help of understanding parents, copes with a move, a new baby sister and several less dramatic but familiar events.

Stevenson, James. *What's Under My Bed?* Greenwillow Books, 1983. Ages 4-7.
> Grandpa shares his experiences as a young child in order to help Mary Ann and Louie cope with their nighttime fears.

Willoughby, Elaine Macmann. *Boris and the Monsters.* Houghton Mifflin, 1980. Ages 4-7.
> A small boy masters his fear of the dark when he moves to protect something more helpless than he is – a frightened puppy.

Zalben, Jane Breskin. *Norton's Nighttime.* William Collins Publishers, 1979. Ages 2-6.
    A young raccoon named Norton wanders away from his pine tree and cannot find his way
    home before nightfall. Small children will understand Norton's feelings of fear and insecurity
    and will laugh with relief as the raccoon discovers his friends.

Fear of Being Lost

Mauser, Pat Rhoads. *How I Found Myself at the Fair.* Atheneum, 1980. Ages 7-9.
    An only child, used to her mother's close supervision, goes to a state fair with the large,
    unruly family of a friend and gets lost. After a succession of frightening experiences, Laura
    uses her head and finds her friends again.

Parenteau, Shirley. *I'll Bet You Thought I Was Lost.* Lothrop, Lee & Shepard Co., 1981. Ages 5-8.
    A trip to the supermarket with his father becomes a scary adventure when little Sandy gets
    lost. He tries hard to find something familiar in the people and products he sees, but his panic
    steadily increases until he finds his father; then the boy is delightfully plucky and brave.

Wittels, Harriet and Griesman, Joan. *Things I Hate.* Behavioral Publications, 1973. Ages 4-8.
    This story centers on the fear of getting lost and is a good discussion starter.

Fear of Death

Bunting, Anne Evelyn. *The Big Red Barn.* Harcourt, Brace & Jovanovich, 1979. Ages 4-7.
    In this first-person story, the family barn symbolizes the permanence and security a young boy
    longs for after the death of his mother and the arrival of his stepmother. When the barn is
    destroyed, the boy feels doubly threatened. Through the help of his grandfather, he comes to
    accept the new barn and his new stepmother.

Byars, Betsy Cromer. *Goodbye, Chicken Little.* Harper & Row, 1979. Ages 9-11.
    In this fast-moving story, a quiet, cautious boy comes to grips with several disturbing events
    and emotions: grief and guilt over the accidental deaths of close family members; confusion
    about a friendship; anxiety about his place in an outgoing, often unpredictable family.

Engel, Diana. *Eleanor, Arthur, and Claire.* Macmillan, 1992. Ages 4-8.
    Claire Mouse loves spending summers with her grandparents, Arthur, who makes pottery, and
    Eleanor, a painter. Together they picnic, bake and garden, and their tradition of expressing
    love is to exchange homemade gifts. When Arthur dies, Eleanor is devastated. Finally, she and
    Claire mourn Arthur and begin anew.

Hyde, Margaret and Lawrence. *Meeting Death.* Walker, 1989. Ages 10-17.
    A book about loss that teaches young people about death as part of life. The authors tell that,
    ultimately, understanding death helps us develop an appreciation for life.

Jackson, Jacqueline. *The Taste of Spruce Gum.* Little, Brown & Co., 1966. Ages 10-13.
Eleven-year-old Libby is confused by the sudden changes in her life:moving to a new home and her mother's relationship with another person after the death of her father. The characterizations and human relationships are timeless.

Viorst, Judith. *The Tenth Good Thing About Barney.* Atheneum, 1971. Ages 4-8.
With the aid of supportive parents, a young boy deals with the anxieties and grief surrounding the death of his pet cat.

Fear in General

Blume, Judy. *Otherwise Known as Sheila the Great.* E. P Dutton, 1972. Ages 9-12.
Ten-year-old Sheila is afraid of dogs, water, stange noises and imaginary creatures. Rather than admit her fears, she conceals them through constant boasting and lying. With the help of a friend and her parents, she admits her fears and begins to cope with them.

Berry, Steve. *The Boy Who Wouldn't Speak.* Annick Press. Ages 4-8.
Owen is a boy who never speaks. Never. Not a word. He loves to play, has plenty of good friends and likes to smile, but he won't speak. After befriending two giants, Owen appoints himself peacekeeper.

Carlson, Nancy. *What if it Never Stops Raining?* Puffiri, 1992. Ages 5-8.
Tim is a worrier. When it rains, he worries about floods. At school, he worries he'll forget his report card. During a baseball game, he worries he'll strike out. But somehow things have a way of working out – not always perfectly, but never as badly as Tim thinks they will.

Coles, Allison. EDC Publishing. Ages 3-7.
Michael's First Day at School. 1984.
Michael in the Dark. 1984.
Michael and the Sea. 1985.
Mandy and the Hospital. 1985.
Mandy and the Dentist. 1985.
Michael and Mandy are two very normal children and, like every child, they are sometimes afraid of the unknown. These stories show how Michael, Mandy, and many others overcome their fears and enjoy life more fully for having been brave.

Crofford, Emily. *A Matter of Pride.* Carolrhoda Books, 1981. Ages 8-11.
A young girl learns what courage can entail through her mother's brave overcoming of her fears in the interest of protecting her family and preserving their few possessions during the Depression.

Heck, Bessie Holland. *Cave-In at Mason's Mine.* Charles Scribner's Sons, 1980. Ages 8-10.
A young boy must overcome his fears and practice the new skills his father has taught him in order to save his father's life in this suspenseful adventure.

Macdonald, Maryann. *Sam's Worries.* Disney, 1990. Ages 3-7.

Sam can't fall asleep, and he begins to worry – about a volcano under his house, cobras in his garage and the lunch lady at school being a witch. Sam's bear understands and offers to do Sam's worrying, so Sam can sleep. Young bedtime worriers will find comfort in this unique solution to common childhood fears.

Pfeffer, Susan Beth. **What Do You Do When Your Mouth Won't Open?** Delacorte Press, 1981. Ages 10-13.

A young girl with a deep fear of public speaking is helped to overcome her phobia in this lively first-person narrative. Although it seems odd that Reesa has never received help from parents or teachers and must seek it out herself, her encounters with the psychologist are convincing and the book's other relationships and situations ring true.

Tester, Sylvia Root. *Sometimes I'm Afraid.* Children's Press, 1979. Ages 3-5.

A small child describes some of her fears and explains how she has become less fearful. Children will understand that fears are a normal and sometimes even necessary part of life.

Fear of Physical Harm

Andersen, Karen Born. *What's the Matter, Sylvie, Can't You Ride?* The Dial Press, 1981. Ages 4-7.

Fear prevents Sylvie from learning to ride her new bicycle. Only when she gets reckless, so frustrated and angry that the possibility of physical harm is momentarily unimportant, does she conquer the bike. Though aimed at young readers, this story captures that familiar struggle between the drive to succeed and the fear of failure.

Cohen-Posev, Kate. **How to Handle Bullies, Teasers and Other Meanies.** Rainbow Books, 1995. Ages 8-14.

This book provides information on what makes bullies and teasers tick, how to handle bullies, how to deal with prejudice and how to defend oneself when being teased or insulted. Among other things, it covers annoying name-calling, vicious prejudice, explosive anger, dangerous situations and causes of difficult behavior. It gives dozens of examples and practice exercises to teach a comic approach to cruelty.

Farmer, Patti. *What Do You Think I Am— Crazy?* Barron's, 1991. Ages 4-7.

Little duck doesn't want to take a walk because he might break a leg. He doesn't want to swim because he might drown, and he doesn't want to fly because he might break his neck. Then winter comes, and the family flies south. But not stubborn little duck—not until the winds begin blowing, and he finds himself alone.

Petty, Kate and Firmin, Charlotte. *Being Bullied.* Barron's, 1991. Ages 4-7.

Rita is bullied by Bella, another girl at school, but finds relief when she stands up to her. Her mother helps her find the courage to deal with situations that can be understood by many children, but it's no match for a brave cowgirl with a lasso who is out to stop it.

Schmitt, Christine. *It Takes Courage.* Paulist Press, 1995. Ages 10-14.

> Savannah discovers her new friend from summer camp is a victim of child abuse and by offering trust and support helps the girl and her family begin the healing process. "Telling" becomes the best thing Julia could have done.

Fear of School

Delton, Judy. *A New Girl at School.* E. P. Dutton & Co., 1979. Ages 4-7.

> Nervous about going to a new school, a little girl finds the adjustment difficult at first, but before too long, she begins to make friends and feel at home. Soon, there's a newer student than she.

Gross, Alan. *The I Don't Want to Go to School Book.* Children's Press, 1982. Ages 5-9.

> This humorous look at a boy trying to evaluate the pros and cons of going to school will appeal to any reader who has ever had a bad day at school.

Hogan, Paula Z. *Sometimes I Don't Like School.* Raintree Publishers, 1980. Ages 6-9.

> Embarrassment about his poor performance in arithmetic clouds a young boy's feelings about school. He tries desperately to avoid the situation entirely; however, his understanding teacher recognizes his need for help. Once George admits his problem, he can does take the necessary steps to solve it.

Lasker, Joe. *Nick Joins In.* Albert Whitman & Co., 1980. Ages 5-8.

> A disabled child's initial fear of school dissolves with barely a ripple, thanks to understanding parents, sympathetic teachers and his own outgoing attitude.

London, Jonathan. *Froggy Goes to School.* Viking, 1996. Ages 4-7.

> It's the first day of school, and Froggy is more than a little nervous. When he tries to pour the milk on his breakfast bowl of flies, the carton falls out of his hands. Will he ever pull himself together in time to make it to the classroom?

Quackenbush, Robert M. *First Grade Jitters.* J. B. Lippincott, 1982. Ages 5-7.

> In this short, simple tale of apprehension about school, the young rabbit narrator feels defensive when his parents try to define his jitters.

Russo, Marisabina. *I Don't Want to Go Back to School.* Greenwillow Books, 1994. Ages 6-9.

> Summer is over, but second-grader Ben doesn't want to go back to school. All he can think of are the terrible things that might happen. No one will remember him, or he'll forget to get off the bus on the way home. However, things don't turn out as Ben expects.

Tester, Sylia Ross. *We Laughed a Lot My First Day of School.* Children's Press, 1979. Ages 3-6.

> A Mexican-American boy discovers that his fears about kindergarten are unfounded, and he enjoys a positive first day experience.

Thaler, Mike. ***The Principal from the Black Lagoon.*** Scholastic, 1993. Ages 5-10.
> A humorous story about every child's fear of a visit with the principal. Another appropriate story is *The Teacher from the Black Lagoon.*

Fear of Separation

Bourgeois, Paulette. ***Franklin is Lost.*** Scholastic, 1992. Ages 4-7.
> Franklin is back in this cautionary tale about the dangers of straying too far and the renewed security of coming home.

Helmering, Doris Wild. ***I Have Two Families.*** Abingden Press, 1981. Ages 6-8.
> This timely first-person narrative, told by Patty, shows that children can live a normal life after their parents' divorce. Patty and Michael experience all the fears and uncertainties that most children of divorce feel.

Marcus, Irene and Paul. ***Into the Great Forest: A Story for Children Away from Parents for the First Time.*** Magination Press, 1992. Ages 5-7.
> This delightful fairy-tale, dream story details the insecurity and anger children may feel toward their parents when facing a separation. Through identification with the main character of this story, children can realize and use their own strengths and capabilities to face the unknown.

Molnar, Dorothy and Fenton, Stephen. ***Who Will Pick Me Up When I Fall?*** Whitman, 1991. Ages 4-7.
> A working mother's young child who spends each day after school with someone else, needs Mommy's reassurance of love. She thinks that Mommy will go off to work and forget about her.

Schuchman, Joan. ***Two Places to Sleep.*** Carolrhoda Books, 1979. Ages 5-7.
> David is uncertain and fearful about his parents' divorce. Despite patient, supportive and reassuring parents, the young boy needs time and abundant love to accept the break-up of his family.

Weninger, Bridgette. ***Good-bye, Daddy!*** North-South Book, 1995. Ages 5-8.
> Tom is sad and angry when he comes home after a day out playing with his daddy. This tender story-in-a-story makes the emotionally charged topic of separation and divorce approachable. Even though it ends on a sweet and hopeful note, the story offers no simple solutions or contrived happy endings.

Fear of Storms

Sussman, Susan. ***Hippo Thunder.*** Albert Whitman & Co., 1982. Ages 3-6.
> A little boy learns a simple and relatively accurate trick for overcoming his fear of thunder.

Zolotow, Charlotte. *The Storm Book.* Harper & Row, 1952. Ages 5-9.
> The scariness and eventual beauty of a storm and its aftermath are described to help the young reader cope with fear of storms.

Fear of the Unknown

Calhoun, Mary Huiskamp. *The Night the Monster Came.* William Morrow & Co., 1982. Ages 5-10.
> Andy "cries wolf" several times before the monster he sees, a wounded bear, impels him to consider the safety of others as he overcomes his fear and traps the animal.

Hogan, Paul Z and Kirk. *The Hospital Scares Me.* Raintree Publishers, 1980. Ages 3-8.
> This reassuring and simple yet informative account of a little boy's surgery and hospital stay could help prepare children for a hospital visit or be useful in describing the hospital experience to a child's siblings or classmates.

Lankton, Stephen. *The Blammo-Surprise! Book: A Story to Help Children Overcome Fears.* Magination, 1988. Ages 6-11.
> The story begins with Terry's fear of the circus. It continues with a dialogue between Terry and Knowsis, which arouses positive feelings and uses them to eliminate the fear. A surprise ending helps children make the learning part of their own self-concept.

Lipp, Frederick J. *Some Lose Their Way.* Atheneum Pulbishers, 1980. Ages 10-13.
> Two lonely young 8th graders find their way past the misconceptions they have about each other to form an enduring, nourishing friendship. Natural history becomes an integral part of the story.

Mayer, Mercer. *There's Something in My Attic.* Puffin Books, 1988. Ages 4-8.
> When a big, noisy nightmare lives in the attic right over your head making creaking sounds when you're trying to sleep and even stealing your toys when you aren't looking, something must be done. That big nightmare may look and sound scary...but?

Tregebov, Rhea. *Sasha and the Wind.* Second Story Press, 1996. Ages 5-9.
> Sasha loves the way the wind sails kites and turns umbrellas inside-out. He wants to be blown so high that the people below look like chocolate chips. Then one day the wind no longer acts like a playful friend. A fire alarm forces Sasha's class outside, where the wind seems to be bullying the anxious children. A warm, funny story about overcoming fear.

Wartski, Maureen Crane. *The Lake is on Fire.* The Westminster Press, 1981. Ages 5-9.
> A boy's numb despair over his own blindness and death of his friend lifts when he embarks on a dangerous trek through a burning forest, forced to rely on the eyes of the dog he fears.

Appendix I-D: Resource List

In addition to the numerous references throughout the book, the following may be helpful when it comes to specific treatment of anxiety and fear-related disorders:

Dwivedi, K. N., & Varma, V. (1997). *The handbook of child anxiety management.* Bodmin Great Britain: Hatrnoll, Ltd.

Jasenka, R. (1995). *LA '94 earthquake in the eyes of children: Art therapy with elementary school children who were victims of disaster.* Journal of American Art Therapy Association, 12, 37-43.

King, N. J., & Ollendick, T. H. (1997). *Annotation: Treatment of childhood phobias.* Journal of Child Psychiatry and Psychology, 38, 389-400.

Ollendick, T., & King, N. (1994). *Diagnosis, assessment and treatment of internalizing problems in children: The role of longitudinal data.* The Journal of Consulting and Clinical Psychology, 62, 918-925.

Books

Benson, P.L., Galbraith, M.A., Espeland, P. (1998). *What kids need to succeed.* Search Institute and Free Spirit Press, 400 First Ave. North, Suite 616, Minneapolis, MN 55401-1724, (800) 735-7523, help4kids@freespirit.com and www.freespirit.com.
Based on research, this book spells out 40 developmental assets young people need to succeed and offers checklists and 900 specific, concrete suggestions to help a child build assets at home, at school, in the community and in the congregation.

Benson, P.L., Galbraith, M.A., Espeland, P. *What teens need to succeed.*
More than 1200 ideas for helping adolescents build developmental assets, 120 true stories, 200 resources (books, organizations and websites), checklists and quizzes

Brenner, A. (1984). *Helping children cope with stress.* Lexington, MA: Lexington Books, $10.95.
For teachers and those who work with children under stress.

Canfield, J., & Wells, H. (1976). *100 ways to enhance self-concept in the classroom: A handbook for teachers and parents.* Paperbacks for Educators, 426 West Front Street, Washington MO 63090, $21.95.
K – adult: Self-esteem building activities.

Cox, E. (1996). *Why I am special.* Career Track Publications, 3085 Center Green Drive, Boulder, CO. 80301. 303/440/7440.
Simple esteem-building activities for children 8 and under. Useful for teachers or parents.

Doyle, P., & Behrens, D. (1986). *The child in crisis.* Paperbacks for Educators, 426 West Front St., Washington, MO 63090, $17.95
For teachers/ counselors to help children cope with personal crisis.

Dreyer, S. (1985). *The bookfinder: When kids need books.* American Guidance Service, Publishers Building, Circle Pines, MN 55014; $19.95 softcover; $54.95 hardcover.
Reference volume of children's books by author, title and topic or subject.

Faber, A., & Mazlish, E. (1980). *How to talk so kids will listen and listen so kids will talk.* Paperbacks for Educators, 426 West Front St., Washington, MO 63090, $6.95.
For parents, teachers, counselors and administrators.

Fredericks, M., & Segal, J. (1979). *Creative puppetry in the classroom.* Rowayton, CT: New Plays Books.
Illustrations and instructions for puppet making.

Graver, C. M., & Morse, L. (1986). *Helping children of divorce: A group leader's guide.* Springfield, IL: Charles C. Thomas, $19.75.
For educators and counselors to help elementary students cope with divorce.

Gregson, B., (1982). *The incredible indoor games book.* Paperbacks for Educators, 426 West Front St., Washington, MO 63090, $11.95.
Grades K-8: Guidance, team-building, communication and cooperation.

Kuhn, M.A. (1992). *Coming to terms with divorce: A guided support program.* Center for Learning. Available from Social Studies School Service, 10200 Jefferson Boulevard, Room M711, Culver City, CA 90232-0802, (800) 421-4246, www.socialstudies.com.
A book for the child, *Mom and Dad Break Up,* and a companion book for adults which includes dialogues, games, art exercises, puzzles and response activities helpful for parents, teachers or counselors working with children ages 5-12.

Lesesne, T. S. (1986). *I'm special: A program for 4th graders.* The Drug Education Center, 1416 E. Morehead, Charlotte, NC 28204, $9.50.
Grades 3-5: Unit of activities to build self-esteem, communication and decision-making skills.

McCullough, C. J., & Mann, R. W. (1985). *Managing your anxiety.* Jeremy P. Tarcher, Inc., 9110 Sunset Blvd., Los Angeles, CA 90069, $15.95.
Stress management

McKnew, D. H., Jr., Cytryn, L., & Yahraes, H. (1983). *Why isn't Johnnie crying? Coping with depression in children.* W. W. Norton, 500 Fifth Ave., New York, NY 10110, $15.50.
Depression in young children.

Myrick, R., & Bowman, R. (1981). ***Becoming a friendly helper: A handbook for student facilitators.*** Educational Media Corp., Box 21311, Minneapolis, MN 55421, $4.95.

Children helping children: Teaching students to become friendly helpers. Educational Media Corp., Box 21311, Minneapolis, MN 55421, $9.95.
Grades 5-8: Peer counseling, manuals for trainers and students.

Renfro, N. (1979). ***Puppetry and the art of story creation.*** Austin, TX: Nancy Renfro Studios.
Comprehensive, illustrated guide to puppetry.

Robinson, J. (1985). ***Culture shock: Information packet for developing stress/culture shock programs for students in overseas schools.*** ERIC Document Reproduction Service No. ED 249430.

Sarafino, E. (1985). ***The fears of childhood: A guide to recognizing and reading fearful states in children.*** Human Sciences Press, 72 Fifth Ave., New York, NY 10011-8004, $3.95.
For teachers and administrators

Stanish, B. (1982). ***Connecting rainbows.*** Paperbacks for Educators, 426 West Front St., Washington, MO 63090, $8.95.
Grades 3-8: Self-esteem, values, cooperation and communication.

Stroebel, C. F. (1982). QR: ***The quieting reflex.*** New York: Berkley Books.
Relaxation training

Thomas, M. (1987). ***Free to be...a family.*** Paperbacks for Educators, 426 West Front St., Washington, MO 63090, $19.95 hardcover.
For use with all ages in school or at home. Contains poems, songs and stories about belonging.

U.S. Department of State. (1986). ***Managing children during a crisis.*** Washington, DC: Author.

Walczak, Y., & Burns, S. (1984). ***Divorce: The child's point of view.*** Harper & Row, 28 Tavistock St., London, UK NC2E7PN, $8.00.
Children's reactions to divorce

Weinstein, M, & Goodman, J. (1980). ***Playfair: Everybody's guide to noncompetitive play.*** Paperbacks for Educators, 426 West Front St., Washington, MO 63090, $9.95.
Grades 4-adult: Team-building and cooperation

Wiseman, A. S. (1989). ***Nightmare help.*** Ten Speed Press, P.O. Box 7123, Berkeley, CA 94707
A helpful book for parents, teachers and counselors to guide individual children to find solutions for their dreams and nightmares. Includes background information on dreams, nightmares and fears. Also includes 27 casework examples of children's dreams/nightmares with the child's illustrations.

Multimedia

Active parenting (1999). Active Parenting Publishers, 810 Franklin Court, Suite B, Marietta, GA
30067, www.activeparenting.com.
A comprehensive parent education program for parents of young people from birth through
high school. Leadership training, video/book series available in English, Spanish, Japanese,
and Korean.

Antonucci, P., Schumacher, S., & Travers, L. (1986). *Biofeedback microlab.* HRM Software, Room
MI-78910, 175 Tompkins Ave., Pleasantville, NY 10570, $350.00 for disk, interface box,
sensors and guide.
Grades 6-adult: For students/teachers to provide firsthand feedback to the body's reaction to
stress.

Bowman, R. P. (1987). *Test buster pep rally.* Educational Media Corp., P.O. Box 21311,
Minneapolis, MN 55421, $79.95.
Grades K-6: Test-taking strategies and stress reduction.

Christensen, B., & Vanderslice, C. (1984). *Who am I? Looking at self-concept.* Sunburst
Communication, Inc., 39 Washington Ave., Pleasantville, NY 10570-9971, $109.00
2 filmstrips/2 cassettes: Self-esteem enhancement.

Coping with family changes. Sunburst Communications, 101 Castleton St., Pleasantville, NY
10570-9971, $165.00.
Grades 6-9: Filmstrips/cassette or videocassette

Davis, D. E. (1988). *My friends and me.* American Guidance Service, Circle Pines, MN 55014-
1796, ranges from $12.95 to $285.00 for entire guidance kit, components separate.
Guidance kit: 4, 5 and 6 year olds

Dinkmeyer, D., Sr., & Dinkmeyer, D., Jr., (1982). *DUSO Revised: Developing understanding of
self and others.* American Guidance Service, Circle Pines, MN 55014-1796, $149.00 to
$249.00.
Guidance kit: Grades 6-9

Dupont, H., & Dupont, C. (1979). *Transition.* American Guidance Service, Circle Pines, MN
55014-1796, $242.50.
Guidance kit: Grades 6-9

Dupont, H., Gardner, O. S., & Brody, D. S. (1974). *TAD: Toward affective development.* American
Guidance Service, Circle Pines, MN 55014-1796, $249.00.
Guidance kit: Grades 3-6

Einstein, E. I., & Albert, L. (1986). *Strengthening step-families.* American Guidance Service, Circle
Pines, MN 55014-1796, $89.50.
Parent education program with audiotapes and other components: 5-session program

Hendricks, G. *The centered student: Stress & relaxation.* Learning Tree Filmstrips, P.O. Box 4116, Englewood, CO 80155, $99.00.
Grades 3-6: 8 audiocassettes and guide: self-confidence, creativity and handling stress

Herzfeld, G., & Powell, R. (1986). *Coping for kids: A complete stress control program for students ages 8-18.* Center for Applied Research in Education, P.O. Box 430, West Nyack, NY 10995, $39.95.
Managing stress

Kuhn, M.A. (1992). *Coming to terms with divorce: A guided support program.* Center for Learning. Available from Social Studies School Service, 10200 Jefferson Boulevard, Room M711, Culver City, CA 90232-0802, (800) 421-4246, www.socialstudies.com
A book for the child, *Mom and Dad Break Up*, and a companion book for adults that includes dialogues, games, art exercises, puzzles and response activities helpful for parents, teachers or counselors working with children ages 5-12.

Learning to say no. (1985). Sunburst Communications, 101 Castleton St., Pleasantville, NY 10570-9971, $119.00 filmstrip/cassette; $139.00 videocassette.
Grades 4-6: Refusal and assertiveness skills

Lions-Quest, *Skills for Growing* (1998). Quest International, P.O. Box 4850, Newark, OH 43058-4850, 800/446-2700, http://www.quest.edu.
Developmental K-5 program focusing on life skills, drug prevention and character education. Includes training for facilitators of the program and a parent connection component.

Lions-Quest, *Skills for Adolescence* (1996). Quest International, P.O. Box 4850, Newark, OH 43058-4850, 800/446-2700, www.quest.edu.
Developmental 6-8 program focusing on developing life competencies through and emphasis on character education, communication and decision-making skills, and service-learning.

Palmer, H. (1973). *Sea gulls* [Recording]. Freeport, NY. Educational Activities.
Background music for relaxation

Popkin, M. H. (1983). *Active parenting.* American Guidance Service, Circle Pines, MN 55014-1796, $295.00.
Parenting education program with videocassette and other components: 6-session program.

Stroebel, E., Stroebel, C. F., & Holland, M. (1980). *Kiddie QR: A choice for children.* QR Institute, 119 Forest Drive, Wethersfield, CT 06109.
Relaxation training tapes and manuals

Thomas, M. (1979). *Free to be…you and me* [Recording]. New York: McGraw Hill.
Songs to learn about self and others

Part II

Coping with Trauma

Section 1

Helping Children in a Time of Crisis:

Coping with Traumatic Events

Helping Children in a Time of Crisis: Coping with Traumatic Events

Introduction

The terrorist attacks that befell the United States on September 11, 2001, psychologically and emotionally affected individuals everywhere. Certainly, the events and the aftermath deeply impacted Americans. Traumatic events that affect adults often have a tremendous effect on children who look to the adults in their lives for security and stability. For children who witnessed the event directly or vicariously through media coverage, symptoms of distress such as tears, fears, anger, sadness, confusion, and bad dreams are normal. It is important to help children cope with these normal reactions to prevent clinical problems and to recognize the elements of severe psychological distress, which may need immediate clinical treatment.

In this section, we will provide an overview of helping children to cope with traumatic events, what constitutes trauma in a child's life and how to recognize the symptoms of distress that may result from trauma. We will also discuss some of the possible effects of trauma on children including Post Traumatic Stress Disorder. Additionally, specific strategies for parents, teachers, counselors, and other mental health providers will be outlined for use in prevention and treatment.

What is a Traumatic Event?

A traumatic event is any event or incident to which a child is exposed, either directly or indirectly through vicarious means, that is outside the range of typical experience and which has the potential to overcome the child's normal ability to deal with the stress that results from the exposure to or participation in the event. These events might include physical or sexual assaults, accidental physical injury, death or loss of property, terrorist attacks, natural disasters, etc. In essence, any event could be a critical incident that is traumatic for an individual child. The severity of the trauma and the subsequent distress is dependent on a number of variables that tend to be individual in nature. These might include the child's previous experience with trauma, the level of security that the child typically feels, and the number and nature of relationships with family, adults, and peers. In addition, the general mental health of the child and his or her sense of self-worth and self-concept impact the level of distress. Finally, the child's sense of control over his or her life and the number and degree of skills in handling stress and anxiety in general affects the child's ability to cope with a traumatic event.

Common Signs of Distress

Signs of distress that are often found following exposure to traumatic events include physiological symptoms, cognitive reactions, emotional responses, kinesthetic reactions, and behavioral reactions. Physiological reactions might include nausea, upset stomach, chest pains, dizziness, chills, loss of coordination, tremors, muscle aches, numbness, headaches, increased heart rate, and palpitations. It is important that a physician examine any physical symptoms if they persist over time or are severe in nature in order to eliminate any physical issues whose onset may have coincided with the critical incident.

Cognitive reactions that may occur include abreaction or seeing the event over and over again in the mind's eye, slowed thinking and confusion and difficulty with problem-solving and making decisions. Other symptoms that may be seen include difficulty concentrating on tasks or engaging in activities that were previously mastered, difficulty in naming familiar objects, or difficulty recalling names. Perhaps one of the most common symptoms is hypervigilance, often manifesting itself in excessive checking and securing. Emotional reactions that may be noted include a general increase in emotional expression or a reduction in emotional expression such as withdrawal or displaying flat affect. Other common emotional responses include sadness, feelings of guilt, anger, fear, grief, and depression.

Behavioral reactions might include a change in eating habits, which might be manifested in an increase or decrease of food intake, or a change in sleeping habits whether sleeping more than usual, less than usual, or increased nightmares. Temper tantrums and anger outbursts or other rapid changes in mood including bouts of crying that were not common previously are also possible symptoms of distress as are any marked changes in behavior. Bad dreams and night terrors are also common reactions to the stress of trauma.

While the above is an accurate reflection of the type of symptoms that are common reactions to distress, it may be helpful to look at how this might be seen in children specifically. Young children may display such regressive behaviors as thumb sucking, wetting the bed, waking in the night, wanting to sleep in the parents' room, and outbursts of anger or bouts of crying when separated from caretakers(s) where previously they had adjusted to this separation. Older children may complain of being down or appear lethargic, lower their risk-taking behaviors, complain of bad dreams or night terrors, find it difficult to sleep, or spend more time avoiding sleep to the point of exhaustion. Another indication is a change in play habits often including acting out the trauma or events surrounding the trauma. This could be seen in play with dolls or toys or on the playground in role-playing games of children.

Post-Traumatic Stress Disorder in Children

Post-Traumatic Stress Disorder (PTSD) is defined as the development of characteristic symptoms following exposure to an extreme traumatic stressor involving direct personal experience of an event that involves actual or threatened death or serious injury or other threat to one's physical integrity; or witnessing an event that involves death, injury, or a threat to the physical integrity of another person; or learning about an unexpected or violent death, serious harm, or threat of death or injury experienced by a family member or close associate (APA, 2000). Post-Traumatic Stress Disorder is perhaps the most common disorder that results from trauma in a crisis situation (Yule, Perrin, & Smith, 1999). For the DSM-IV-TR description and diagnostic information, see Appendix I-B.

Mediating Elements in a Crisis

Different children will react differently in a crisis situation. Not all children who have been exposed to a trauma will develop symptoms of distress or more problematic behaviors or disorders such as Acute Stress Disorder (ASD) or Post-Traumatic Stress Disorder (PTSD). For more information on these disorders, see Appendix I-B.

Some factors that will make a difference, including the degree of distress experienced or whether or not the distress becomes problematic, include such variables as how the child experienced the trauma or the other resources of the child such as the child's emotional health or the level of support, the reactions of adults, and previous exposure to trauma.

How the child experiences the trauma can affect the impact that the trauma may have on the child. There is some evidence that children who are directly involved in the incident may be more strongly affected than someone who is vicariously experiencing the trauma (Lindeberg, Jones, Collard, and Thomas, 2001). The rule of thumb is that those children most directly involved and those children closest to the violence are more likely to experience difficulties (Webb, 2002).

The inner resources of the child can mediate the effects of the trauma; the developmental level of the child can have an impact (Crosser, 1994); and the sense of control, self-worth and security can also be factors. The latter is particularly important with regard to the ability to develop and maintain a support system of family, friends and adults in their world. Children who feel that they have a strong support network are less likely to develop problems.

How adults react to the crisis can be an important mediating factor as children look to see if the adults around them are able to handle their own distress surrounding the crisis. Finally, the general level of functioning of the family system also exists as an important mediating factor in a crisis (Linares et al., 2001). Children will also notice if parents, teachers, counselors, and school psychologists are able to engage in appropriate defusing activities with children during or shortly following the trauma (NASP, 2002).

The child's mental health, emotional health, physical health, and exposure to previous trauma can affect the child's reactions to a crisis incident where trauma is individual. Children with previous exposure to trauma are more likely to develop ASD and/or PTSD associated with the crisis. Exceptional children may have difficulty in a crisis (Friehe & Swain, 2002).

Historical Perspective on School Crisis Response

The history of crisis response on the part of schools with regard to traumatic incidents is spotted with inconsistency. One of the first incidents of a traumatic event that received nationwide attention occurred in Chowchilla, California, in the early 1970s (Terr, 1981). Children were kidnapped and buried underground in their school bus and were left for twenty-seven hours to ponder their situation before they were rescued. The school or community did not provide any special services for helping the children mediate the distress resulting from the incident. Terr (1981) reported that in a follow-up with the children five years later, all the children had developed clinical symptoms including depression and anxiety.

As a result of Chowchilla, some schools and school districts began to develop crisis teams to help children and families deal with such events. Poland (1994) outlines a series of events that have shaped the crisis response efforts including the bomb explosion in Cokeville, Wyoming, shootings in an elementary school in Winnetka, Illinois, and shootings at Cleveland Elementary School in Stockton, California. Since then, school violence in Barnwell, South Carolina; Jonesboro, Arkansas; Columbine, Colorado; and Paduka, Kentucky have taught us at least two things. Schools that have a crisis plan and intervene with appropriate mental health services directly following a critical incident have a positive effect in helping children deal with the distress of the trauma and preventing later problems. Secondly, we have learned in light of past events and those of September 11, 2001, that no school is isolated from trauma. One recent study indicates that over 50% of children in urban settings are exposed to traumatic events in situations of daily living (Sweatt, Harding, Knight-Lynn, Rasheed, & Carter, 2002). All schools should have a plan to deal with such crises. Several resources exist to help schools to develop an appropriate plan for dealing with crises.

Helping People Cope With Tragedy and Grief, edited by Garry Walz and Chris Kirkman (2002), offers information useful in helping children in a crisis including information for families, teachers and counselors. The book also provides a comprehensive list of resources helpful in a crisis such as children's literature and web links to other resources. It outlines suggested ways to help parents and teachers help children, tips and resources for counselor and mental health professionals and handouts/guides for parents.

Preparing for Crisis in the Schools: A Manual for Building A School Crisis Response Team (Brock, Sandoval, & Lewis, 2001) provides an overall guide to preparing for a crisis in the school from school board policies to specific strategies and action steps.

Crisis Intervention Handbook: Assessment, Treatment and Research (Roberts, 2002), provides an excellent overview of crisis theory and interventions. This book also includes specific models for Critical Incident Stress Debriefing (CISD) and Critical Incident Stress Management (CISM). Additionally, there are chapters on assessment and intervention with children and adolescents.

Other resources can be obtained from professional organizations. The American Counseling Association provides online resources for the public through their website (http:www.counseling.org).

Crisis Planning

While the discussion identifies resources offer a tremendous array of other resources, most come up short in one area. They do not stress the importance of pre-planning and continuous updating of the crisis plan, which are considered critical factors to managing crisis situations. The greatest problem in linking appropriate services to children in a crisis stems from gaps in the delivery plan. Arrangements should be made up front with community agencies if they will be needed. Administrators, teachers, counselors, school psychologists, students and parents must know what their roles are in a crisis and in the aftermath. It is the little details that are important. Have all school staff been trained in crisis response? Have parents been consulted, and do they know what the school will do and what they will ask parents to do in a crisis? Have school board members, parents, and community stakeholders been sold on the plan? Have schools shared the research on best practices so that precious time is not lost in deciding what an appropriate intervention is for the crisis? The research suggests that time is an important factor when implementing Critical Incident Stress Debriefing (CISD) (Campfield & Hills, 2001). Do parents know that play therapy techniques are effective for crisis reponse counseling (Webb, 2001) or that CISD is an effective crisis intervention (Everly & Boyle, 1999)? Do parents know they should deal with their own distress because their level of anxiety can mediate the stress of their child in crisis and trauma situations (Linares, Heeren, Bronfman, Zuckerman, Augustyn & Tronick, 2001) or that debriefing is important for children with disabilities and special needs (Friehe & Swain, 2002; Lavoie, 2002; NASP, 2002)?

It is extremely important to provide all stakeholders with the information they need to understand particular strategies and techniques used in responding to a crisis. During a crisis, individuals are not always able to make good decisions in a hurry. The crisis interventions should be automatic and mutually supported. Perhaps the most important mediating elements over which control can be exercised deal with interventions prior to and following the crisis. Planning ahead and helping children develop good coping skills is foremost in preventing long-term problems. Following a traumatic event, defusing activities are the first level of intervention. Following this, Critical Incident Stress Debriefing and Critical Incident Stress Management should be implemented.

Defusing Activities

Defusing activities are those activities that help children express their emotions surrounding the crisis, communicate their fears and anxiety about what they believe is or was happening, and implement coping skills including assessing the support networks they have to deal with the crisis and their reaction to the trauma. Activities include information sessions to discuss what happened and to sort out fact from fiction and rumors. The activities also help children find a safe place to express feelings verbally or nonverbally using journals, art, music, drama, etc. Activities that promote normalization, reduce tension and determine future needs are stressed (McNally and Soloman, 1999).

Critical Incident Stress Debriefing

Following defusing activities on the broadest scale, it is important to begin Critical Incident Stress Debriefing (CISD) with those individuals most likely to be negatively affected by the trauma (Mitchell, 1983). Critical Incident Stress Debriefing is defined as a meeting of those involved in a traumatic event with the goal of diminishing the impact of the event by promoting support and encouraging processing of traumatic experiences in a group setting (Richards, 2001). Evidence suggests that CISD helps to prevent the development of Acute Stress Disorder and Post-Traumatic Stress Disorder. Research also suggests that the sooner CISD is instituted following the trauma the more effective it is in preventing problems. We have included a quick guide in Appendix II-D to outline the steps associated with the Adapted Family Debriefing Model for CISD in this publication because it is an adaptation designed for children, schools, and families.

Critical Incident Stress Management

Critical Incident Stress Management (CISM) refers to a systematic individual intervention for persons exposed to a traumatic event. CISM might include Critical Incident Stress Debriefing as a part of a broader intervention (Bohl, 1991; Chemtob, Tomas, Law, and Cremniter, 1997). Critical Incident Stress Management may begin after Critical Incident Stress Debriefing for those individuals who show signs of developing Acute Stress Disorder and/or PTSD, or it can be used as a preventative strategy. In addition to the use of CISD as a part of CISM, other strategies offered to individuals in CISM are stress inoculation training, cognitive behavior therapy, and other individual intervention techniques for counseling (Richards, 2001).

References

American Psychiatric Association. (2000).*Diagnostic and statistical manual of mental disorders* (4th ed., text revision). Washington, DC: Author.

Bohl, N. (1991). The effectiveness of brief psychological interventions in police officers after critical incidents. In J. Reese, J. Horn, & C. Dunning (Eds.), *Critical Incidents in Policing – Revised.* Washington, DC: US Government Printing Office.

Campfield, K. M., & Hills, A. M. (2001). Effect of timing of critical stress debriefing on posttraumatic stress disorder. *Journal of Traumatic Stress, 14*(2), 327-340.

Chemtob, C. M., Tomas, S., Law, W., & Cremniter, D. (1997). Debriefing and crisis intervention. In D. Black, M. Newman, J. Harris-Hendricks, & G. Mezey (Eds.), *Psychological Trauma: A Developmental Approach*, pp. 238-249. London:Gaskill.

Crosser, S. (1994). When young children are afraid. *Day Care and Early Education*, 7-11.

Everly, G. S. (1995). The role of the critical incident stress debriefing process in disaster counseling. *Journal of Mental Health Counseling, 17*(3), 278-300.

Everly, G. S., Jr., & Boyle, S. H. (1999). Critical incident stress debriefing: A meta-analysis. *International Journal of Emergency Mental Health, 1*(3), 165-168.

Friehe, M. J., & Swain, K. D. (2002). Helping students with disabilities deal with acts of terrorism. *Communication Disorders Quarterly, 23*(2), 87-90.

Juhnke, G. A. (1997). After school violence: An adapted critical incident stress debriefing model for student survivors and their parents. *Elementary School Guidance & Counseling, 31*(3), 163-170.

Lavoie, R. D. (2002). Walking them through the horror: Talking to your child about the world trade center tragedy. *Communication Disorders Quarterly, 23*(2), 103-104.

Linares, L. O., Heeren, T., Bronfman, E., Zuckerman, B., Augustyn, M., & Tronick, E. (2001). A mediational model for the impact of exposure to community violence on early child behavior problems. *Child Development, 72*(2), 639-652.

Lindeberg, M. A., Jones, S., Collard, L. M., & Thomas, S. W. (2001). Similarities and differences in eyewitness testimonies of children who directly versus vicariously experience stress. *The Journal of Genetic Psychology, 162*(3), 314-333.

McNally, V. J., & Solomon, R. M. (1999). The FBI's critical incident stress management program. *FBI Law Enforcement Bulletin*, February 1999, 20-26.

National Association of School Psychologists. (2002). Coping with terrorism-helping children with special needs: Tips for school personnel and parents. *Communication Disorders Quarterly, 23*(2), 100-102.

Poland, S. (1994). The role of school crisis intervention teams to prevent and reduce school violence and trauma. *School Psychology Review, 23*(2), 175-189.

Richards, D. (2001). A field study of critical incident stress debriefing versus critical incident stress management. *Journal of Mental Health, 10*(3), 351-362.

Roberts, A. R. (Ed.). (2000). *Crisis intervention handbook: Assessment, treatment, and research* (2nd ed.). Belmont, CA: Wadsworth.

Sweatt, L., Harding, C. G., Knight-Lynn, L., Rasheed, S., & Carter, P. (2002). Talking about the silent fear: Adolescents' experiences of violence in an urban high-rise community. *Adolescence, 37*(145), 109-120.

Terr, I. C. (1981). Trauma aftermath: The young hostages of Chowchilla. *Psychology Today, 15*(4), 29-30.

Walz, G. R., & Kirkman, C. J. (Eds.). (2002). *Helping people cope with tragedy and grief.* Greensboro, NC: ERIC Counseling and Student Services Clearinghouse.

Webb, N. (2002). *Helping bereaved children: A handbook for practitioners* (2nd ed.). NY: Guilford Press.

Webb, P. (2001). Play therapy with traumatized children: A crisis response. In G. Landreth (Ed.), *Innovations in play therapy: Issues, process, and special populations.* Philadelphia, PA: Brunner-Routledge.

Yule, I., Perrin, S., & Smith, P. (1999). Post-traumatic stress disorders in children and adolescents. In I. Yule (Ed.), *Post-traumatic stress disorders: Concepts and therapy.* Chichester, England: John Wiley and Sons, Ltd.

Section 2

Trauma-Specific Activities

Introduction

This section on trauma-specific activities is designed to help mediate the effects of such traumatic events in a child's life as natural disasters. Disasters such as hurricanes, tornadoes and earthquakes can be equally as traumatic to the individual child as death of a parent, an accident, bodily injury, and a house fire. Ideally, these activities should be done before major symptoms appear as a part of prevention for those children exposed to traumatic events. However, these activities may also be integrated into treatment after symptoms are present. Finally, some of these activities may address specific prevention areas and fears as covered in Part I, Sections 2 and 3, so the reader should use professional judgment and consider integrating these activities into fear-prevention while also considering what activities from Part I may also benefit the trauma-exposed child.

Felt Art Fun

Trauma Area:	Any Trauma
Curricular Area:	Counseling
Grades:	K-2
Size:	Individual
Time:	30 minutes
Purpose:	To help discover the fear source and overcome it.

Outcomes:

The students will be able to:
1. Trust and confide in the counselor through playing with the felt dolls;
2. Identify the fear source;
3. Discuss the event or situation that caused the fear;
4. Develop coping skills to deal with the fear if it occurs again.

Materials:

1. Felt-covered board
2. Different colored felt material
3. Glue
4. Scissors

Procedures:

1. Give the student different colors of felt material, glue and scissors.
2. Instruct the child to cut out the people in his/her family including pet(s).
3. After the child has cut out the characters, ask him or her to put the characters on the felt board and tell a story about something that has frightened him/her. The counselor can prompt the child with such questions as, "How does mommy doll feel about that?" or "How do you feel about that?" The counselor should adapt the questions to each child's particular story and/or situation.
4. Give suggestions to the student on how to cope and deal with the fear(s) if they should happen again. This activity can be used for any issue. The child will have the freedom to move the characters around the felt board with ease as he/she tells the story. The hope is that the child will feel safe in disclosing his/her fears though the use of the felt dolls when telling the story.

Using Children's Literature

Trauma Area:	Any trauma
Curricular Area:	Language Arts
Grades:	K-8
Size:	Full class
Time:	30 minutes
Purpose:	To help children realize that others share the same fears and to help them cope with their fears.
Outcomes:	*The students will be able to:* 1. Identify the character's fear after listening to the story; 2. Discuss their own experiences with this fear; 3. Identify ways the character coped with his/her fear; 4. Generate ways of coping with this fear the next time it is encountered.
Materials:	A story selected from the *Bibliography of Books About Children's Fears* (see Appendix I-C) or another story which addresses a childhood fear and in which the character(s) is/are able to cope with his/her fear.

Procedures:	1. Introduce the story and read it to the children. Ask them to listen for what the characters are afraid of and what the character(s) does/do when he/she is afraid.
	2. Discuss the story with the children. Ask the children to talk about:
	    a. The character and what the character was afraid of;
	    b. Times they have experienced a similar fear;
	    c. How they felt inside when they were afraid;
	    d. What the character did in the story to cope with his/her fear;
	    e. What they do to help themselves when they are afraid;
	    f. What they might do the next time they experience this fear.

Discussion of the story is the crucial part of this activity. It provides opportunities for students to share how they would feel, think and act in a similar situation and learn how the story character or other peers would cope with the same situation

Art Exploration

Trauma Area:	Any trauma
Curricular Areas:	Language Arts, Science, Art, Social Studies
Grades:	K-8
Size:	5-20 students
Time:	As many class periods as needed
Purpose:	To help students express anxieties and fears related to a disaster or tragedy they may have experienced directly or through the media

Outcomes:

The students will be able to:
1. Depict experiences through art media;
2. Talk about their experiences, thoughts and feelings related to the event;
3. Begin to resolve thoughts and feelings of the trauma and cope with related fears.

Materials:

1. Paper
2. Markers
3. Crayons
4. Colored pencils
5. Pastels
6. Charcoal
7. Tempera paint
8. Finger paints
9. Clay
10. Play dough

Procedures:

1. Encourage students to draw a picture of the disaster or tragedy the way they remember it. Use questions that stimulate their thought processes such as:
   a. Where were you?
   b. What happened?
   c. What did you do?
   d. Who was with you?
2. In subsequent class times, encourage students to elaborate on their pictures or draw other pictures. Some children may resist or refuse to draw pictures related to the event and may choose instead to draw events from safer, pre-trauma times. Some children's drawings may focus on familiar media or fantasy heroes who could defeat anything. Others may regress in their style of drawing to an earlier developmental time in childhood. Others may displace the event actually experienced with another traumatic type of event. All are normal expressions and should be encouraged.
3. Initial drawings should have little direction from the counselor, teacher, parent or other helpful adult, but in later drawings, the student can be encouraged to create a safe place in their drawings or include persons who might come to their aid. Humor should also be encouraged as well as those parts of the experience that were happy such as the family being unharmed and all together even if their home was destroyed. Some students may pursue factual information about natural disasters such as tornadoes and include that information in their artwork.

4. During and after the art experience, time should be provided for students to verbalize what is being depicted in their pictures and asked to talk about their feelings and behaviors during the event. The facilitator of the group discussion should reflect successful coping strategies, identify supportive people in the child's life as well as ideas for handling similar experiences. The facilitator can also elaborate with information about ways to relax when anxious or fearful, reverse negative thoughts into positive and explore additional outlets for expression of feelings.

Personal Crisis Management

Trauma Area:	Any trauma
Curricular Area:	Counseling
Grades:	K-8
Size:	Individual, group, full class
Time:	Varies
Purpose:	To help children express feelings and thoughts related to a personal crisis event and develop coping strategies that may be helpful in coping with a crisis situation.
Outcomes:	*The students will be able to:* 1. Define the meaning of crisis; 2. Identify feelings and thoughts related to experiencing a crisis; 3. Discuss actions that would be helpful to take in a crisis situation; 4. Generate steps that can be taken when facing a personal crisis.
Materials:	1. Chalkboard or 2. Flip chart and marker
Procedures:	The occurrence of a personal or situational crisis in an elementary child's life may impair normal emotional functioning. These crises could include death of a relative or friend, divorce or separation, neglect, abuse, parent's loss of a job, moving abroad, experiencing a different culture for the first time, terrorist acts and illness or accident.

1. Individual:

Listening to a student who is experiencing a personal crisis and creating an accepting, nonjudgmental atmosphere helps the student unlock feelings and express thoughts, anxieties, or fears related to the situation. Rather than give advice, the teacher can serve as a mirror reflecting back to the child the feelings and thoughts expressed. The child may not wish to communicate verbally. Just being with someone who cares about him/ her may help the child feel more secure. Playing games, drawing or reading a book together are other ways of expressing care and concern for the child.

2. Small Group: Small group discussion led by a teacher may be a mode of support for children experiencing a common crisis or similar situation. Participants in a group learn that they are reacting naturally, which can reduce their feelings of loneliness and of being different. For example, children who share the common experience of their parents' divorce may express similar feelings, recognize common situations, hear other's coping strategies and find support and help through the phases of adjustment. Goals of a small discussion group should include helping the children express feelings, understanding what happened and why, and deciding what action can be taken to cope with the crisis.

3. Classroom Guidance: A classroom guidance approach can be a means of helping children who are experiencing a personal crisis to develop adaptive coping behaviors as well as provide each of the students with an opportunity to develop coping skills before a crisis event occurs. The following classroom guidance approach can be divided into several lessons:

a. Using a brainstorming technique, lead the children toward formulation of a composite definition of the word "crisis." Fill the chalkboard or a chart with as many crisis events that can happen to a student as they can generate.

b. Ask the students to select a crisis event that happened to them or someone they know, and draw a picture about the event and/or write a story about it. Younger children may choose drawing and older children may prefer to write. Allow enough time for the children to thoroughly develop their writings or drawings.

c. Encourage the students to share their writings or drawings with the class including any details of the event or feelings elicited by the event that they wish to share.

d. Use the brainstorming technique again to identify various feelings experienced during a personal crisis. Also, ask the students to brainstorm some of the things they think about during a crisis event.

e. It is important to include an action phase in the classroom guidance approach. Lead the students to a discussion of action strategies using the following questions:

> *What did you do that helped you in a time of crisis?*
> *Who might help you in a time of crisis?*
> *What steps might you take to help yourself if you are facing a crisis event?*

f. As a means of culminating the classroom guidance approach, the teacher should formulate a summarization of the main points of the lessons and allow the students to summarize what they have learned about handling a crisis situation in their life.

4. Taking time to structure a small group discussion or classroom guidance approach will help the teacher recognize some of the personal struggles of their students. It may also help identify students and families who may benefit from more professional help and with whom the teacher may want to remain in closer communication. Schools need to recognize the effects personal crises have on students and learning and perhaps develop policies for dealing with children in crisis.

Collective Crisis Management

Trauma Area:	Any trauma
Curricular Area:	Counseling
Grades:	K-8
Size:	Full class
Time:	Varies
Purpose:	To help students cope with the stress and fear due to collective crises which may occur in or around the school.
Outcomes:	*The students will be able to:* 1. Express and accept their fears; 2. Gain a realistic sense of security in relation to a crisis; 3. Remain reasonably in control in relation to a crisis.
Materials:	The booklet, *Managing Children During a Crisis*, U.S. Department of State, February 1986.
Procedures:	1. *Guidelines for Adult Behavior:* Collective crises are rare (but, unfortunately, real) occurrences that affect groups of people, such as a class, a school or an entire community, rather than individuals or isolated families. These crises include accidents, kidnappings, bomb scares and bombings, coups, insurrections, riots and acts of terror. Although the incidence of such crises is low, it is best for teachers, counselors and administrators to be prepared for such eventualities and to be aware of certain generally accepted guidelines for dealing with a collective crisis.

In the case of a crisis, school personnel should do the following:

    a. Be in contact with the parents of the children involved as soon as possible. A free flow of information will serve to calm the fears of both groups and will add to the children's feelings of security;

    b. Not avoid discussion of the incident. To feel fear after a dangerous incident is natural. Children (and adults) need an outlet for their feelings and fears. To ignore the incident will make the children feel that there is something wrong with them for feeling as they do;

    c. Remain calm. Children will look toward adults and adult behavior for security in times of crisis. Panicky adults will only lead to loss of control on the part of the children. Be reassuring and comforting, with liberal use of physical contact;

    d. Be honest and forthright with children. Give supportive information that will build up trust between you and the child. It is better to say, "I don't know" than to deliberately make up something that will later prove false;

    e. Mobilize the child's own resources. Encourage children to help each other, to talk, to sing, to play games or whatever else is appropriate for lifting spirits and distraction. Allow students to help with chores, clean up, distribute food, etc.— all things that will permit them to feel in control.

2. **Activities During a Threat Period:** During periods of stress due to social, political or environmental factors, teachers, counselors and administrators should discuss the following:
    a. Roles and tasks of each staff member during the crisis;
    b. Communication/information systems such as radios, telephone networks, emergency channels, etc.
    c. First aid procedures;
    d. Stress management and relaxation techniques for periods of confinement;
    e. Adult fears and communicating to children about fears and other emotions;
    f. Preparation for post-violent incident classroom activities;
    g. Procedures for evacuation from school.

3. **Classroom Activities Following a Crisis:**

    a. Unfinished sentences:

During the _____ , I was scared when _____ .
When I heard that _____ , I felt _____ .
I still think about _____ .
When I (see, pass by, hear) _____ , I think about _____ , and I feel _____ .

    b. Drawings to accompany sentences

Pictures of what happened
People it happened to
Yourself [the child] at the time
Composite picture of event on a large board or mural

    c. Re-enacting the event with children (or puppets, dolls, etc.) taking the roles

    d. Teacher-led discussions

Who did what and why
What they might have done
What we know now that we didn't know then

    e. Poems, stories, songs, letters, assemblies, discussions and drills dealing with the event or similar events

Source: U.S. Dept. of State. (1986). *Managing children during a crisis.* Washington, DC: Author.

Systematic Desensitization

Trauma Area:	Any trauma
Curricular Area:	Counseling
Grades:	K-8
Size:	Individual
Time:	30-45 minutes
Purpose:	To help students deal with their unreasonable fears.
Outcomes:	*The students will be able to:* 1. Relax when faced with feelings of fear; 2. Control their fears so as to be able to enter into the activities of the school.
Materials:	A hierarchy of situations related to the client's fear.

Procedures: Mental health professionals use systematic desensitization as a technique to treat clients who experience unreasonable emotional reactions, such as intense fear, when confronted with situations that are not dangerous in and of themselves. This technique is especially useful in the treatment of common phobias, such as the fear of heights, claustrophobia, and the fear most commonly found in students, school phobia.

The technique focuses on pairing relaxation behavior with mental images of fear-inducing stimuli organized in a graduated hierarchy. In other words, the client is told to imagine things that approximate more and more to the phobic situation that he fears in real life while at the same time relaxing. By mixing fear-producing situations with relaxing behavior, the technique gradually breaks down the association of the feared object with the fear response because a person cannot be tense (a physiological response to fear) and relaxed at the same time.

1. The first step is to construct a hierarchy of images that are related to the client's fear or phobia. The hierarchy should begin with something that is only remotely connected to the fearful situation and then, in gradual approximations, the images should become more and more similar to the actual fear. For example, if a student has a fear of going to school, one could start with something relatively benign, such as getting up in the morning. Then, one could progress gradually through all the steps that lead to going to school itself. Finally, one can arrive at the school.

2. The second step is to teach the client relaxing behavior (see Relaxation Scripts, pp. 177). The relaxing behavior must be taught to the client before beginning to introduce the hierarchy so that relaxation can be paired with the mental images.

3. What follows is a script of a session of systematic desensitization with a ten-year-old who, because of his father's frequent job changes, must change schools often. Unfortunately, he has a fear of meeting new people that has generalized to a case of school phobia. Three different levels of the hierarchy will be presented:

Counselor: "Last time we talked about how you get very nervous about meeting kids at school. You've explained to me how you feel scared at the thought of starting a conversation with someone whom you don't know. You said that your palms start to sweat, your heart begins to beat faster, and you feel short of breath and uncomfortable. The only way that you have been able to control this reaction is to avoid the situation and stay by yourself. You said that it has become so bad that you don't even want to go to school anymore. Is that about right?"

Student: "That's right."

Counselor: "OK, you also said that despite these feelings, what you really want is to feel comfortable enough at school with other students to make friends. We agreed that with your family moving around so much, and you having to attend different school so frequently, it's a real pain not to be able to make friends comfortably like the other kids. Would you say that describes how you feel?"

Student: "Yes."

Counselor: "Great. Well, we can work on this problem by using a procedure with a fancy name – desensitization. By using desensitization, those situations that make you feel tense and nervous now will no longer cause you to feel bad. The procedure has been used very successfully with thousands of people all over the world to help them reduce their fears of certain situations. I feel it can work with you, too."

"To make this work, you will first learn how to relax. After you're relaxed, I ask you to imagine some things about meeting people, starting first with things that aren't too frightening, and gradually thinking about more uncomfortable situations. As we go along, the relaxation will start to replace the tension and fear, and some of the things that you might think are stressful now will no longer seem so bad later. Do you have any questions about this?"

[The first stage in the hierarchy]

Counselor: "OK, now that you've learned how to relax, it's time to try some desensitization. I'm going to ask you to imagine something. Listen to what I say and try to put a picture of it in your mind. At the same time, just remain relaxed and calm. If you start to feel tense, I want you to raise your pointing finger of your right hand. Let's try that now."

"Great. All right, now relax as we've just been practicing. Imagine you're lying down in a grassy field on a calm, peaceful day. The sun is warm, and there's a gentle breeze blowing on your face. You're just so comfortable lying there that you feel like you're just melting into the grass. The tenseness is leaving your body. You're breathing deeply, and the air feels so fresh and clean. You're calm and relaxed, and you feel so good.

"Good. Now imagine you are home, and you overhear your parents talking. Your father is telling your mother that he might be transferred to another job and that you might have to move again. You don't know if you will have to move; there is only the possibility that you will have to. Imagine that conversation and keep that image in your mind. Just think about it for a while." *[Wait for 10 seconds]*

"OK, now go back to your relaxing. You didn't raise your finger, which means that you didn't feel very tense, right?"

Student: "Right."

Counselor: "Good. Let's do it again." *[Repeat the scene]*

"That's great. You got through that without any trouble. Let's try another.

[Skipping several steps in the hierarchy]
Counselor: "OK, you've been doing just fine so far. Let's try another one. Now just relax and imagine the next scene that I describe to you. It's the first day at your new school, and you are getting in the car with your mom to go to school. You are opening the door and just getting in, you sit down next to your mom, and your mom starts the car. You pull away from the curb..."

Student: *[Raises his finger indicating fear.]*

Counselor: "OK, just relax. Think of...*[Go back to the relaxation scene]* That's it. Breathe deeply. Feel relaxed?"

"Let's try it again." *[Repeat the same scene. If no fear response, go on to the next step in the hierarchy.]*

[Skipping several steps in the hierarchy]

Counselor: "All right. We've gone through a whole list of scenes, and you've managed to stay calm and relaxed throughout the process. Let's give it one more try with a new scene. Now relax again as we practiced."

"You're at school, and the teacher has just let the class out for recess. You're on the playground, and the boys are getting up a game of volleyball. You want to play too, but in order to do so, you have to go over to one of the guys and ask him to let you in on the game. You are walking over to him to talk to him, you are figuring out what you want to say, and he turns around to look at you. Think about that, keep it in your mind and relax."

Student: *[Raises finger indicating fear]*

Counselor: "OK, relax." *[Bring up the relaxation image again and terminate the session after achieving relaxation.]*

Drawing In A Friend

Trauma Area:	Any trauma
Curricular Area:	Counseling
Grades:	K-8
Size:	Full class
Time:	60 minutes
Purpose:	To help students learn to identify coping strategies.

Outcomes: *The students will be able to:*
1. Identify fearful situations;
2. Express and accept their feelings;
3. Identify people, objects or places that help them cope with feelings of fear.

Materials:
1. Drawing paper
2. Colored pencils or crayons

Procedures:
1. Begin discussion of remembering times of feeling fearful.
2. Discuss with students what fear feels like and its effects on the body.
3. Allow students to draw out a situation where they remember feeling fear.
4. After drawing the fearful situations, ask students to share with the group about the situation.
5. After each student has talked about his/her drawing, ask him/her to begin a new drawing that includes the situation of fear and include what could make the situation less fearful or easier to get through. Ask them to draw in friends, objects or thoughts that would help them cope with the situation.
6. Ask each student to share with the group his/her second drawing and what made the situation easier to get through.

Visualizing Help

Trauma Area:	Any trauma
Curricular Area:	Counseling
Grades:	K-8
Size:	Full class
Time:	15 minutes – Designed to follow activity "Drawing In A Friend"
Purpose:	To help students learn self-nurturing and relaxation techniques and to help develop awareness of coping strategies.

Outcomes:

The students will be able to:
1. Identify coping strategies
2. Implement relaxation techniques

Materials:

1. Tape or CD player
2. Relaxation music
3. Drawing from the activity entitled "Drawing In A Friend"

Procedures:

1. Ask students to visualize the new situation that they drew during the previous activity, including the friend or the help that made the situation easier to get through.
2. Play the music for 15 minutes, asking the class to enjoy the music while relaxing their bodies. They should imagine the situation happening and visualize their friend with them and change the scene so that it is not fearful.

Writing to My Fear

Trauma Area: Any Trauma

Curricular Area: Language Arts, Art

Grades: 4-8

Size: Full Class

Time: 20 minutes

Purpose: To help students learn to identify feelings of fear, develop a sense of control over the feelings, and express feelings associated with fear.

Outcomes: *The students will be able to:*
1. Identify sources of fear;
2. Recognize that these feelings of fear come from within;
3. Control these feelings.

Materials: 1. Writing paper
                        2. Pencils or pens

Procedures: 1. Begin discussion of situations where the students felt fear.
2. Ask students to write a story about a little girl or boy who felt scared.
3. When stories are finished, ask the students to share what their stories are about.
4. Ask students to write another story but include something that would help the situations to be less scary.

Hurricanes and Floods

Trauma Area:	Hurricanes, Floods
Curricular Areas:	Science
Grades:	4-8
Size:	Full class
Time:	30 minutes
Purpose:	To help children cope with a fear of hurricanes and floods and to appreciate how nature responds before, during, and after natural disasters.

Outcomes:

The students will be able to:
1. Express their fears in a group setting;
2. Discuss their past experiences with hurricanes and floods;
3. Explain how a hurricane builds and flooding occurs;
4. Describe ocean creatures and other animals before a hurricane;
5. Describe the animals' safe place during the hurricane;
6. Describe a safe place for the child during a flood;
7. Discuss the aftereffects of a hurricane or a flood;
8. Generate ways to cope with this fear the next time it is encountered.

Materials:

1. Rubber animals or sea creatures from oceans, lakes, and low-lying coastal areas
2. Book on how hurricanes form and affect sea and land animals

Procedures:

1. Allow each child to select one animal and one sea creature for this exercise. Ask them to imagine where each might be located when a hurricane approaches land.
2. Read book aloud to children, stressing where sea and land animals go for safety.
3. Discuss the actions of the creatures and humans in preparing for a hurricane or a flood. Ask the students to talk about the following:
   a. Where creatures go to seek shelter and safety;
   b. Where humans go to seek shelter and safety;
   c. Some problems humans face during a hurricane;
   d. What humans can do during a hurricane;
   e. What problems land animals face with a flood;
   f. What humans can do for safety with a flood;
   g. What the children do during hurricane season to cope;
   h. What the children might do the next time they experience this fear.

ERT (Emergency Response Team) Careers

Trauma Area: Natural disaster (flood, hurricane, tornado, fire) or violent event (school shooting, bombing)

Curricular Areas: Social Studies, Language Arts, Health/Science, and Career Education

Grades: 5-8

Size: Small group or full class

Time: 120 minutes (several class periods)

Purpose: To help children recognize that many adults are available and willing to help others in emergency situations.

Outcomes: *The students will be able to:*
1. Name the types of workers in helping careers who respond to people's needs in emergencies.
2. List the personal qualities that people need when working in the helping careers.
3. Identify the job responsibilities of specific helping careers.
4. Discuss ways that these helpers relieve people's fear, stress and suffering.

Materials:
1. Newspapers or magazines
2. Scissors
3. Glue
4. Paper
5. Large index cards

Procedures:
1. Introduce and discuss emergency or crisis situations.
2. Make a list of these situations (i.e., flood, hurricane, tornado, earthquake, fire, bombing, shooting)
3. Direct the students to work in groups of three to find an example of one real emergency in recent news magazines or newspapers.
4. Assign the task of listing the types of jobs in each career cluster that would be needed to respond to their emergency situation. See example below.

Examples:

Communication/Media	**Health Care**	**Military**
News reporter	Paramedic	Helicopter pilot
Public Service	**Transportation**	**Environmental**
Firefighter	Truck driver	Meteorologist
Personal Service	**Law Enforcement**	**Volunteer**
Counselor	Victim's Assistance	Red Cross worker
Minister	Investigator	

5. List the education level (high school, college, post college) needed for each job. List the personal qualities that the people who do these jobs must have (i.e., kind, caring, understanding, responsible, helpful, patient, persistent, dedicated, decisive, hard-working, etc.)

6. Assign each group the task of developing three "Guess Who" cards to read aloud.

Example:

I am needed when there is a _____ type of emergency.

One of my job responsibilities is to _____ .

I need a _____ education to do this job.

One personal quality I have is _____ .

7. Play the "Guess Who" game.

8. Discuss specific ways that the assistance of these workers helps to relieve people's fear, stress and suffering.

Pictures of Me

Trauma Area: Any trauma

Curricular Area: Counseling

Grades: 6-8

Size: Full class

Time: 60 minutes

Purpose: To help students understand how they view themselves in different areas of their lives.

Outcomes: *The students will be able to:*
1. Project through tangible objects how they see themselves
2. Dispute any negative self-concepts
3. Focus on positive traits

Materials:
1. Several different magazines and newspapers
2. Scissors
3. Tape or glue
4. Construction paper

Procedures:
1. Have the students select a picture for the following levels of expression: emotional, physical, social, spiritual, mental.
2. Have the stude2nts assemble and tape or glue pictures into a collage onto the construction paper.
3. Ask the students to share with the class what their pictures represent.
4. Discuss the reasons why they see themselves as what is represented in the pictures.
5. Ask the students to dispute any negative self-concepts presented.
6. Discuss the importance of positive self-concepts.

Web Sites

The following Web sites may be helpful in understanding childhood fears and anxiety disorders. They may be used to collect further information for the reader or as resources for parents and others.

http://www.sover.net/~schwcof/ptsd
>Bibliography of Post-Traumatic Stress Disorder

http://www.npi.ucla.edu/caap/
>Child and Adolescent Anxiety – UCLA

http://www2.mc.duke.edu/pcaad/
>Anxiety Disorders in Children – Duke University

http://www2.hawaii.edu/~chorpita/casap
>Child Anxiety

Section 3

Stress-Reducing Activities

Introduction

Stress-reducing activities are those activities that might be better described as stress management. The goal of these activities is to help children manage both distress and eustress; in other words, those emotions and tensions that are generated around negative stimuli as well as those around positive stimuli. Children have become just as stressed at the joy of Christmas and Hanukah as to the pressure of taking a high stakes test. These activities are meant to help children mediate their stress in ways that provide relief from the related effects. Other activities in this section are designed to prevent stress from creating debilitating effects in the child.

Five-Minute Stress Relievers

Treatment:　　　　　Stress

Curricular Areas:　　At any opportune time during the day

Grades:　　　　　　K-4

Size:　　　　　　　Full class

Time:　　　　　　　5 minutes

Young children experience varying degrees of tension that may be the result of feelings of fear or anxiety in their everyday life. General worry throughout the day as well as a temporary "uptight" feeling can hamper academic and social development. Often the adults in a child's life (parents, teachers, etc.) can control the situations or conditions a child experiences and, whenever possible, should find ways of altering the situation to make it less stressful for the child.

Teachers can use quieting tricks and exercises to reduce tension and stress in the classroom as well as teach their students something they can utilize anytime they feel the tension begin to build. The idea is to put these quieting tricks into action before stress, tension or anxiety is at a peak.

1. **"Think of Something Quiet."** Raise your voice just slightly and say, *"Look at me. I want you all to think of something very, very quiet. Don't tell me what it is, but I'm going to be able to look at each of your faces, and I'll be able to tell if you're thinking of something quiet."* The children will respond instantly as you search their faces for the relaxed mental state and the whole emotional tenor of the room will change.

2. **"Mr. Nobody."** You can also reduce stress with humor. Open the classroom door and say, *"Oh, hello, Mr. Nobody. Come in."* This grabs the children's attention because they can see no one is there. Place a chair for Mr. Nobody and invite him to be seated. One by one, the children join in fantasy, and this brief dose of whimsy makes for a calmer approach to the remainder of the day.

3. **"Hand Squeeze."** Don't take hand-holding or hand-touching for granted. It's a way of enhancing interpersonal communication skills. Ask everyone to form a circle (sitting or standing) and to hold hands. You begin by gently squeezing the hand of the child to your right, then relaxing your grip. Be sure to reinforce that they should "touch gently." That child then squeezes the hand of the child to his/her right, then relaxes his/her grip. Continue around the circle. Do a few group squeezes in unison and say, "Hold. Squeeze. Hold. Squeeze," for whatever length of time seems appropriate.

4. The following is a quieting activity that can be done in 5 minutes after students finish outdoor play, before beginning a test or any other time when the students may need a quieting activity. This can be done as they sit in a chair or at a desk. The teacher sits in front of the student and, with a calming voice tone, tells the story and demonstrates the motions.

"Canoe Trip Down a Jungle River"

"We are going to take a canoe trip down a quiet jungle river. Let's begin paddling." (Paddle to the left and right)

"Look to the left at the beautifully colored parrots perched on the tree branches." (Look left)

"Look to the right at the amusing monkeys playing in the trees." (Look right)

"We're getting hungry. Let's paddle under that tree ahead to pick some of the fruit that is hanging from those low branches. Pick some fruit with both hands. Take a bit of the sweet, juicy fruit. It tastes delicious. Take another bit. Chew." (Paddle, reach up with each hand, bite and chew)

"Let's paddle on. There are some alligators on the bank to the left of us. Let's paddle more quickly. They're not interested in us. We can slow down." (Paddle left and right slowly and more quickly)

"Oh, our boat has a leak. Get the bucket and start bailing water out of the boat. Take a piece of gum out of your mouth and push it down into the hole until we can fix it properly." (Lean over and bail water over each shoulder. Lean over – push the gum in the hole)

"We're getting tired. Let's stop for a rest under that big clump of trees ahead. Lay your paddle down. It's so cool under these trees. Close your eyes. Listen to the birds calling each other. Feel the coolness of the air. Listen to the water slapping lightly against the boat. Breathe deeply and slowly. Open your eyes. We're ready to go on." (to the next activity, test or whatever) (Hands free in lap, breathe slowly and deeply three times)

Source: *Think of Something Quiet*
By Clare Cherry.

Clay Creations

Treatment:	Stress
Curricular Area:	Art
Grades:	K-6
Size:	Individual or group
Time:	30 minutes
Purpose:	To help children reduce tension and anxiety in their lives through coping skills.

Outcomes:

The students will be able to:
1. Work through anxiety by releasing tension;
2. Identify the causes of the tension;
3. Discuss the experience that caused the tension;
4. Develop coping skills for this tension if they occur again.

Materials:

1. Rolling pin
2. Cookie cutters
3. Plastic knife
4. Clay
5. Toothpicks

Procedures:

1. Give the child a ball of clay (one color to avoid mixing colors). The child can pound as much as he or she wants to release pent-up anxiety and tension.
2. Let the child create whatever objects, figures, food, people, or other items that he or she wants.
3. Let the child talk about what he or she has made and then ask the child to tell a story about something that makes him/her angry or afraid (using the clay creations).
4. After the child has disclosed the particular scene and issue(s), then the counselor can begin to help the child deal with those unfavorable issues. First, the counselor will ask the child to think of ways to handle the situation in the future. Then the counselor will model how to cope and solve problems. The hope is that through the clay activity, the child will relax and use his or her imagination and talk either to the counselor or to himself or herself about whatever is bothering him/her.

Relaxation Exercises and Guided Imagery

Treatment: Stress

Curricular Areas: Any content area

Grades: K-8

Size: Full class

Time: 10-20 minutes

Purpose: To diminish the effect of fears and stress.

Outcomes: *The students will be able to:*
1. Reduce the physical tension in their bodies;
2. Use their imagination creatively to help manage stress;
3. Reduce tension due to fears and stress.

Materials: 1. Relaxation scripts (see following pages)
2. Tape recorder with soft music (optional)

Procedures: 1. Relaxation exercises designed especially for children can help them to
become aware of the feelings of body tension and provide skills to reduce it
Reducing muscle tension seems to help reduce anxiety as well. Using guided imagery
and pleasant fantasies can also help reduce anxiety as well as stimulate children's
imaginations and enrich the learning process in children.
2. Relaxation training and guided imagery can be conducted in a regular classroom or
physical education class, with a large or a small group. Once children develop the skills,
they can use them to relax in many different settings without an instructor. Incorporating
imagery or fantasy with relaxation exercises serves to maintain the child's interest.
3. These general guidelines should be followed:
   a. Use a soft, even voice.
   b. Prepare students to enter a relaxed state as well as leave the relaxed state.
   c. Adjust time according to age level: K-3: 10 to 15 minutes per session; 4-8: 15 to
   20 minutes per session.
   d. Two to three sessions per week will help to establish the exercises with the
   students.
   e. Background music can enhance the effects of the exercises.

A Sharing Circle

Treatment:	Stress
Curricular Areas:	Social Studies, Language Arts
Grades:	3-8
Size:	Full class
Time:	40 minutes
Purpose:	To help students identify what situations cause fear and stress and to discuss coping skills.
Outcomes:	*The students will be able to:*

1. Identify feelings of fear and stress;
2. Communicate feelings of fear and stress
3. Identify common fears among peers;
4. Learn relaxation techniques.

Materials:	None
Procedures:	

1. Introduce the activity to the class and ask members to sit in a circle.
2. Ask members to talk about times whey they felt tension and stress or fear.
3. Ask members to share when they became aware of the tension.
4. Ask members to share what happens to their ability to think straight when they are stressed out.
5. Ask members to share ways they can care for themselves after (maybe even during) a tense situation.

Journal Jazz

Treatment:	Stress
Curricular Areas:	Language Arts
Grades:	4-8
Size:	Full class
Time:	Journal 15 minutes for homework each night for one week
	Art activity 30 minutes
Purpose:	To help children cope with feelings of tension and anxiety.

Outcomes:

The students will be able to:
1. Express their feelings non-verbally;
2. Identify a problem;
3. Demonstrate problem-solving skills;
4. Learn ways to deal with feelings of worry;
5. Practice writing skills.

Materials:

1. Spiral notebook
2. Pen
3. Scissors
4. Colored paper
5. Markers

Procedures:

1. Instruct the student to write down stories in his/her journal on a daily basis for one week as homework.
2. After the week is over, ask the student to choose one of the entries and select a color that fits how he/she feels about a certain story.
3. Have the child use this color to draw a picture describing the journal entry. For example, the child is afraid and worries about his/her alcoholic parent being hurt in a car crash. The child might choose to draw a picture of the car crash.
4. Encourage the child to share his/her feelings about the drawing and help the child deal with the unfavorable feeling and/or event. Some of the following questions may prove helpful to facilitate exploration.
   a. What can you do if you have these feelings of worry most of the time?
   b. What can you do if you feel that you cannot control these feelings?
   c. What can you do to minimize these worries and help yourself to feel more at peace?
5. After the child has come up with his/her own answer, encourage the child with the answers that he/she gives or come up with other alternatives on how to deal with the feelings and/or events. This activity can set the stage for other events that may be worrying the child.
6. This activity is good for children who have a hard time expressing themselves verbally.

Melting Into Music

Treatment:	Stress
Curricular Areas:	Social Studies, Language Arts, Art
Grades:	4-8
Size:	Full class
Time:	20 minutes
Purpose:	To help students learn self-nurturing and relaxation techniques.
Outcomes:	*The students will be able to:* 1. Identify the importance of stress management; 2. Implement relaxation techniques.
Materials:	1. Tape or CD player 2. Relaxation music
Procedures:	1. Begin discussion of the benefits of stress management. 2. Discuss with students what stress feels like and its relationship to illness. 3. Ask the class to sit in a seat and relax their body, sitting quietly with their eyes open or closed. 4. Play the relaxation music for 15 minutes, asking the class to imagine seeing colors that match the music in order to help them relax and feel calm.

Web Sites

The following Web sites may be helpful in understanding childhood fears and anxiety disorders. They may be used to collect further information for the reader or as resources for parents and others.

http://www.geocities.com/~library/Relax
> Index to Relaxation Sites

http://www.tm.org/
> Transcendental Meditation

http://www.uiuc.edu/departments/mckinley/health-info/stress/rela-exe
> University of Illinois Sleep Relaxation Suggestions

http://www.ed.gov/pubs/parents/TestTaking/
> Test Anxiety

http://www.dove.org/columns/1996/column9065
> Stress and TV Violence

http://www.shsu.edu/~counsel/relaxation
> Sam Houston State University Counseling Center Relaxation Page

Section 4

Appendices

Appendix II-A: High-Risk Children in Schools

Some children in schools may experience collective or personal disasters in their lives that can lead to problems related to fears and stress. Inviting such children and other adults in their lives to participate in counseling activities is an important strategy for schools to consider in preventing fear-related problems.

Collective disasters might include earthquakes, tornadoes, hurricanes or a gas explosion that affects a whole neighborhood. In these instances, a large portion of a school population or community may be affected. Such crises remind children that they are vulnerable, raise doubts regarding their sense of security and tend to diminish their sense of control over their own destinies. Although life anywhere is filled with uncertainty, such events can give rise to doubts about their ability to be successful in other areas of their lives and to meet the challenges of daily threats.

Personal disasters, although not necessarily collectively shared, can be just as traumatic for the individual child. Loss of a parent through accident or divorce, bodily injury and trauma of a nocturnal break-in or mugging are examples of personal disasters. These may have the same effect on the child as collective disasters. The child who is under stress from such things as changing schools, family strife, or school failure can also be at greater risk than other children.

The counselor, teacher or administrator may wish to target these children and their families for special intervention. The teachers may be uncertain about what to do. Should they go on as usual? Should they talk about it? What do they say if they do talk about it?

Parents, too, may be uncertain what to do. Often in the face of collective or personal disaster, teachers and parents uncertain about how to broach the topic simply return to business as usual, inadvertently sending the message that this is something not to be explored. In such circumstances, the counselor or administrator needs to help teachers, parents, and children with the opportunity for some release appropriate to the developmental level of the children.

Suggestions

In cases where collective or personal disasters have occurred, teachers should meet with parents first and let them talk out their concerns and fears, then provide them with structured ways they can help children. One suggestion is to have a "sharing time" with the child or children. After the sharing, story time for younger children might help them calm down a bit. One teacher passed out clay during story time. At first, children just kneaded the clay. Later, as their anxiety abated, they began to make things with the clay. Learning how to release the tensions brought on by a crisis situation, then, is the first goal of intervention. Relaxation training, guided imagery, mutual storytelling and other techniques might be helpful follow-up activities. With high-risk populations, the school personnel will want to deal first with the specific issue at hand – allowing for catharsis – then help the children to re-establish their senses of control, self-worth and security.

Appendix II-B: Quick Guide: Things to Do Before a Crisis

Quick Guide: Things to Do Before a Crisis or Traumatic Incident

It is important to be prepared for the crisis before it occurs as much as it is possible. During the crisis, it is often confusing, and individuals with responsibilities have huge pressure not to make the wrong decisions. Depending on the nature of the problem, they may hesitate to enact strategies that will be needed.

The following are intended for use as quick guides and checklists for school staff, teachers, counselors, and parents for dealing with children in a crisis.

1) Is there a board, trustee, or school policy that guides actions during a crisis?
2) Is there a planning or coordinating committee made up of parents, teachers, administrators, counselors, school psychologists, and/or school social service workers, that meet on a regular basis to plan and update the crisis response plan for the district/school?
3) Have key players been identified for dealing with different types of crisis and trauma?
   a. Individual death of a peer or parent
   b. Individual assault in a classroom
   c. Multiple assaults or deaths on school grounds
   d. Multiple assaults or deaths off school grounds
   e. Natural disaster affecting the school
   f. Natural disaster off school grounds affecting the student
   g. Catastrophic event such as a terrorist attack
4) Do key players understand their role in a crisis?
5) Have key players who deal with children, parents, and staff been trained in crisis intervention strategies and are they updated periodically?
6) Have provisions been made to deal with the distress of parents and staff?
7) Have all stakeholders been advised of the types of strategies to be used in a crisis and understand that those strategies are proven and best practices?
8) Are needed materials and resources available for the crisis?
9) Have community resources been identified that will be needed particularly with regard to catastrophic events?
10) Is there a formal agreement with community resources to fulfill a particular role in crisis situations (i.e., school resource officers, mental health agencies, social service agencies, etc.)?
11) Have plans included follow up services to deal with PTSD and other problems that may occur following the crisis?

Please see reference lists for detailed works available to guide this process.

Appendix II-C: Quick Guide: Parents' Guide to Helping Children Cope

Parents Guide to Helping Children Cope with Traumatic Events

As a parent, you may be asking yourself, "What can I do to help my child deal with the traumatic events that they may be exposed to?" The following information may help you with your desire to help your child.

What is a traumatic event?

Any incident that your child sees or is involved in that causes or threatens to cause harm, pain, or loss can be traumatic for the child and may cause the child distress.

Does that mean that my child will have problems because of the trauma?

No, it does not mean that they will have problems, only that they might. Each child is different in his or her ability to handle the stress of a traumatic event. A number of factors can make a difference in whether or not children handle the stress.

What can I do as a parent?

- Parents can moderate their children's sense of distress in a crisis. Children have a keen sense of empathy when it comes to understanding that their primary caregiver is stressed. In a crisis situation, their sense of vulnerability is heightened if they see the adults around them are not in control or are themselves reacting badly to the event. As a parent, you need to deal with your own anxiety surrounding the crisis and try to reassure your child.

- Create a sense of safety and security as soon as possible following the trauma.

- Accept your child's feelings about the crisis. Let them know that emotions such as grief, fear, and anger are a natural response to the situation.

- Listen carefully to your child. Try not to just smooth over their feelings, let them express their emotions. Research shows us that being able to tell this story about what has happened and how they are feeling about it is an important part of dealing with the stress. Don't force your child to talk about it, but invite them. Use open questions like, "What do you think happened? How do you know that? How do you feel about that? What do you think you can do about it?"

- With the "How do you know about that?" question, clear up any misconceptions about what happened. What do we know for a fact? What rumors have we heard? It is important to talk frankly about what happened, so children do not develop misconceptions. For example, you may tell children that there are some bad people in the world that hurt others but most people aren't that way. Then ask them, "How many people do you know who are not that way?"

- Make sure your child knows there are many people available to support them such as parents, other relatives, clergy, teachers, counselors, friends, etc. Let them know it is OK to talk with them as well. Because children feel vulnerable after a crisis, it is comforting to know there is the security of being inside with parents but stress that there are also secure places and place outside of their home.

- Help them develop the skills they need to access help. Children who feel like they have some control over their lives deal better with stress. Teach them who they can go to for help and how to access that person.

- Let your child know that you think things will be OK for you and that you know they will be OK for them, too. Show them you have faith in their ability to deal with the situation. What could you do if this were to happen...? It sounds like you can handle this...It sounds like you have thought about this a good deal...I know you will work it out...

- Learn to recognize the signs of post trauma difficulties such as PTSD. You may be doing all the right things and still have a child that is having a particularly difficult time.

- When you recognize symptoms or problems contact appropriate individuals to get the services your child may need to help them deal with the situation. Your school counselor or school psychologist may be able to help you or put you in touch with appropriate mental health professionals with experience in helping children.

Appendix II-D: Quick Guide: Adapted Family Stress Debriefing

The Adapted Family Debriefing Model (Juhnke, 1997) is an adaptation of Critical Incident Stress Debriefing as proposed by Mitchell and Everly (1993) to address the special needs of children, families, and schools. The model has a twofold purpose of assessment and intervention. In order to maximize the effectiveness of this model, debriefing teams should be established and trained together before the occurrence of a violent episode. The Adapted Family Debriefing Model (AFDM) includes two meetings. The first session focuses on the students' parents and does not include students while the second session is a joint student-parent debriefing experience. Juhnke (1997) recommends that no more than 12 parents be included in a single parent debriefing session. The second session or joint group contains an inner circle of 5-6 students with parents and/or teachers sitting behind them in a larger circle around them to promote unity, support, and stability. As necessary or appropriate, these adults may want to put their hands on their child's shoulders. Trained mental health professionals should act as the leader and co-leader. According to Mitchell and Everly (1993), these sessions should occur within 72 hours of when the student experienced or witnessed the event.

Step 1: Introduction Step
Identify members of team (leaders, co-leaders, doorkeepers)
Explain limits of confidentiality
Remain for entire session
Primary purpose: help student survivors better understand their feelings about the specific terrorist act, increase their coping skills, and gain increased levels of solace

Step 2: Fact Gathering Step
Ask children to report what happened
Child gives name and description of what they first saw or heard
Emphasize telling the *facts* of what each saw or encountered and do not push to describe their feelings (if expressed, indicate as being normal)

Step 3: Thought Step
Transitional in moving from cognitive to affective domain
"What was your first thought when...?"
Validate and normalize each thought and perception

Step 4: Reaction Step
Emotionally charged reaction to the event
"What has been the most difficult part of...?"

Step 5: Symptom Step
Direct from affective back to cognitive
Ask about affective, physical, or cognitive symptoms (i.e., tingling, nausea, trembling hands, inability to concentrate, anxiety)

Step 6: Teaching Step

Possible future symptoms briefly described (recurring dreams, restricted range of affect)...allows to bring up more symptoms as they occur and normalize

"What little things have you done or noticed your friends, teachers, and parents doing that have helped you handle this situation so well?"

Step 7: Re-entry Step

Attempts to place closure on the experience and allows survivors and parents to discuss further concerns or thoughts

Closing comments

Hand-out for student and another for adults discussing common reaction symptoms with 24-hour help line number and work telephone number for the student's school counselor

At the end of this process, the leader and co-leader should encourage parents and students to link with each other for support either through phone calls, e-mails, or meetings in order to continue the understanding and healing process.

References

Juhnke, G. A. (1997). After school violence: An adapted incident stress debriefing model for student survivors and their parents. *Elementary School Guidance & Counseling, 31*, 163-170.

O'Hara, D. M., Taylor, R., & Simpson, K. (1994). Critical incident stress debriefing: Bereavement support in schools developing a role for an LEA education psychology service. *Educational Psychology in Practice, 10*, 27-33.

Mitchell, J. T., & Everly, G. S. (1993). *Critical incident stress debriefing: An operations manual for the prevention of traumatic stress among emergency services and disaster workers.* Ellicott City, MD: Chevron.

Appendix II-E: Resources for Trauma Recovery

Books for Adults

Brooks, B., & Siegel, P. (1996). The scared child: Helping kids overcome traumatic events. New York: John Wiley.

Monahon, C. (1997). Children and trauma: A parent's guide to helping children heal. San Francisco: Jossey-Bass.

National Institute of Mental Health (2000). *Helping children and adolescents cope with violence and disasters*. Washington, DC: NIMH.

Simpson, C. (1997). *Coping with post-traumatic stress disorder*. New York: Rosen Publishing Group.

Books for Children

Alexander, D. W., & Lipson, B. W. (1992*). I can't remember: A story for children feeling the effects of crime or trauma*. Huntington, NY: The Bureau for At-risk Youth.

Alexander, D. W., & Lipson, B. W. (1992). *Something bad happened: A story for children who have felt the impact of crime or trauma*. Huntington, NY: The Bureau for At-risk Youth.

Alpern, M. (2002). *Let's talk: Sharing our thoughts and feelings during times of crisis*. Philadelphia, PA: Chelsea House.

Cohn, J. (1987). *I had a friend named Peter: Talking to children about the death of a friend*. New York: W. Morrow.

Craven, M. (1973). *I heard the owl call my name*. New York: Dell Publishing Co.

Harris, R. H., & Ormerod, J. (2001). *Goodbye mousie*. New York: Margaret K. McElderry Books.

Holmes, M. (2000). *A terrible thing happened*. Washington, DC: Magination Press.

Holmes, M. (1999). *Sam's dad died: A child's book of hope through grief*. Omaha, NE: Centering Corporation.

Holmes, M. (1999). *Ollie's mom died: A child's book of hope through grief*. Omaha, NE: Centering Corporation.

Holmes, M. (1999). *Molly's mom died: A child's book of hope through grief.* Omaha, NE: Centering Corporation.

Jukes, M., & Allen, T. B. (1985). *Blackberries in the dark.* New York: Knopf.

King-Smith, D., & Fisher, C. (1997). *The school mouse.* New York: Scholastic Inc.

Lamb, N. (1995). *One April morning: Children remember the Oklahoma City bombing.* New York: Lothrop, Lee & Shepard Books.

Lawlor, L. (1998). *West along the wagon road, 1852.* New York: Pocket Books.

White, R. (1996). *Belle Prater's boy.* New York: Farrar Straus Giroux.

Websites

Coping with a National Tragedy
National Association of School Psychologists
> http://www.nasponline.org/NEAT/crisis_0911
> This site offers useful information on what to look for in children, what to say, and how adults can help. Current topics addressed include coping with terrorism, promoting tolerance, recognizing severe trauma reaction, managing anger and other strong emotions, preventing suicide, school memorials, children and war, and helping children with special needs cope. Some handouts are translated into other languages.

Helping Children Cope with National Tragedy
National Education Association
> http://www.usnewswire.com/topnews/Current_Releases/0911-130

Coping Resources
National Mental Health Association
> http://www.nmha.org/reassurance/when_to_seek_help.cfm

Coping with Violence and Disasters
National Institute of Mental Health
> http://www.nimh.nih.gov/publicat/violence.cfm
> This site provides information useful in helping children and adolescents cope with violence and disaster.

Guidelines for Children Following Trauma and Disaster
American Psychological Association
> http://www.apa.org/pratice/ptguidelines.html
> This site offers some common reactions that children experience and provides guidelines for children following trauma and disaster.

Resources for Children and Their Parents and Educators Dealing with the Tragic Evens of September 11, 2001
American Library Association
> http://www.ala.org/alsc/dealing_with_tragedy
> This site provides a compilation of materials to aid parents, teachers, and caregivers who wish to discuss with children and teens the terrorist attacks on Tuesday, September 11, 2001.

Teaching Students about Terrorism and Related Resources
> http://askeric.org/Virtual/Qa/archives/Subjects/Social_Studies/Current_Events/tragedy
> A list of resources for educators and parents to help students cope with and discuss terrorist tragedies

Overcoming Crisis
National Center for Kids Overcoming Crisis
> http://www.kidspeace.org/facts

Crisis Communications: Guide and Toolkit
National Education Association
> http://www.nea.org/crisis/
> This Guide and Toolkit provides resources to empower those facing crises and to guide their school communities toward hope, healing, and renewal.

The American Counseling Association Crisis Fact Sheet
American Counseling Association
> http://www.counseling.org/consumers/5ways.htm

Post-traumatic Stress Disorder
National Center for PTSD
> http://www.ncptsd.org/facts/specific/fs_children
> Additional information regarding the signs and symptoms of PTSD in addition to other resources can be found on this website.

The Guidance Channel
> http://www.guidancechannel.com

National Association of School Psychologists
> http://www.nasponline.org

Part III

Facilitator's Guide

Introduction

In order to ensure a successful workshop, it is important to be keenly aware of your audience, their knowledge and sensitivity to the topic, and the way you establish a working relationship with them. One of the best ways to make certain that you are successful is to be as prepared as possible for your workshop. This includes understanding the topic and having a stimulating approach to delivering the material.

Know Your Audience

The participants in your workshop will have a range of experiences in dealing with children's fear and stress. It is important, therefore, not to insult your audience by overstating or undershooting their level of knowledge or skill. This is impossible to avoid 100% of the time, but some ways of checking these extremes exist before beginning or, at the latest, at the beginning of your workshop. First of all, you can use the Fear and Stress Assessment Form (FSAF) included in this guide on page 206 to determine the levels of knowledge regarding the subject and incorporate these results in preparing the agenda of activities. If this is not possible, the instrument or a modified version could be administered as one of the first activities of the workshop. In addition, an agenda-setting time can be spent at the beginning of the workshop which would take into consideration the needs and desires of the participants. This does not mean that you do not come prepared, but it allows for individual differences. You need to operate on the premise of rigid flexibility; rigid to the extent that you have specific goals to achieve and flexible in the way you achieve them.

Eight-Session Design

The eight-session design is intended to accommodate several training configurations. For example, the eight 90-minute sessions can be delivered in a two-day format or as individual sessions after school over an extended period of time. The suggested design can be modified to meet local needs but reducing the time devoted to the total training or a given component could reduce the effectiveness of the preparation. The outline that follows will be presented as a two-day workshop format with the 90-minute blocks defined for easy focus should the facilitator choose an alternative workshop format.

Session 1: Orientation

The purpose of this session is to provide an opportunity for the participants to briefly share something about themselves and establish an atmosphere of relaxed sharing.

The opening session should begin with an introductory activity. You may wish to devise some activity that would involve the entire group to engender some cohesiveness and focus their attention on the topic. If you are working in a school where the staff is small and is well acquainted, a simple go-around activity where you ask each person to share a feeling about being in the workshop and to state why they are interested in the topic is a good beginning. If you are working with a large group or where there are many strangers, a more in-depth get acquainted activity may be needed, such as Human Bingo.

Human Bingo is a fun activity that allows people to discover and share things about themselves and each other by identifying characteristics of others in the group. Each participant is given a Human Bingo card with characteristics identified in each square. Give them 15 minutes to go around the room, identify one person for each characteristic, and ask that person to initial the square that matches the characteristic. The first person that completes the card is recognized and then others are recognized for the number of squares that they completed. The participants are encouraged to obtain as many different signatures as possible. Here is a sample Human Bingo card. You will want to include items of local interest in the blank squares.

Human Bingo

From Northeastern State	Likes Chocolate	Plays Bridge
Likes to Snow Ski	Likes to Exercise	Plays a Musical Instrument
Does Yoga	Has Two Siblings	Has Traveled to a Foreign Country
(ADD YOUR OWN)	(ADD YOUR OWN)	(ADD YOUR OWN)

If the group is acquainted, an activity called "Know Your Place" will both physically energize the group and introduce them to the topic. Know Your Place is an activity that allows the participants to explore their environment, which is often the source of fear and stress. In fact, it is an excellent exercise for use with children. Becoming acquainted with the nuances of one's surroundings can alleviate much potential fear and stress by exposing the fear object for what it is. This activity simply asks the participants to move around the room in silence exploring its contents and composition. Ask them to look under, around, behind, and in things. Ask them to note unusual characteristics about the room and its contents. After 5 minutes of silent exploration, ask them to take a seat and share with the larger group what they discovered. After the discussion ask them, while seated, to take one more sweeping look around the room.

There are many other ways of asking the group to get acquainted with each other and the topic. Be creative and use whatever you think will be effective, but, by all means, include some activity that will set the stage for comfort and sharing.

After the "getting acquainted activity," you are ready to begin your study of children's fears and stress. One of the first items you want to address is the source of one's own fear and stress. It is at this point that the earlier get acquainted activity becomes significant, for the participants are now going to be asked to take greater risks by sharing some of their own experiences with fear and stress. This also helps to personalize the experience while at the same time sharpening awareness of the problems related to fear and stress. This can be accomplished in several ways. However, one way that has demonstrated effectiveness is to encourage teachers to focus on real situations.

With a focus on personalizing the activity, it is necessary for you to be aware of and use the uniqueness of the situation. For example, if you are in an exceptionally contained situation where limits are placed on movement within the community, this may pose different fears and stress than in a more open setting. The activity that follows is intended as an icebreaker and serves as an indirect introduction to the topic. The idea is to get the participants hooked on the subject of fear and stress through tapping their own experience and imagination.

<h1 align="center">Activity</h1>

Title: Fear and Stress Assessment

Purpose: To help participants identify unresolved fears and stress

Outcomes: 1. Recognize how their own fears may be relevant to how they relate to children's fears
                2. Recognize coping strategies used to address fear and stress

Materials: Fear and Stress Assessment Form (FSAF)

Procedures: 1. Ask participants to study the FSAF (see page 206).
                2. Have participants identify a real student fear and stress and complete the form up to the dotted vertical line.
                3. Break group into dyads and ask them to briefly discuss the student fear and stress they identified on the FSAF.
                4. Ask the teachers to reflect upon their own early experiences as they related to the student fear or stress identified on the form and complete the final three sections of the FSAF.
                5. Ask the participants to again discuss their findings in dyads.
                6. Allow time for sharing with the entire group. As this can be a sensitive situation, sharing should be strictly on a voluntary basis.

<h2 align="center">Overview</h2>

After completing the FSAF activity, you will want to give a brief overview of the training and specifically focus on Session 1. At the beginning of each session, it is important to provide an overview. This in itself is an excellent means of allaying some fear or stress with the participants, as was pointed out earlier with the Know Your Place activity. It is also important to conduct a warm-up activity. You will find a suggested warm-up activity at the beginning of each session. Again, these are only suggestions, but it is important that some type of warm-up activity be included.

A suggested overview for Session 1 follows:

"The purpose of today's session is to begin to explore the typical fears and stress of children. You will be asked to voluntarily share some of your own experiences with the topic and how you deal with fear and stress and help children deal with theirs. In addition, we will take some time to discuss a tested model for identifying and treating fear and stress in children. Finally, we will spend some time looking at the sources and signs of stress and fear. In the sessions that follow today, we will be exploring some specific approaches that can be used in the classroom to help children take control of their fear and stress. The classroom suggestions are designed to be infused into the academic curriculum and, therefore, will not add to your already busy schedule. In fact, if implemented, the benefits of helping children deal with their fears and stress can only enhance their focus upon the academic curriculum." You may wish to elaborate on this suggested overview to fit your situation.

Agenda Setting

Since each school setting is unique and the manifested fears and stress are likewise unique, it is important to take time early on during the first session to allow for some agenda setting on the part of the participants. This agenda setting should take place after you have provided the overview. If not, you may not receive any response or you may end up with an agenda that is totally foreign to your purpose. In other words, you need to establish the basic purpose for the training and then, within those parameters, allow for the uniqueness of the setting or individual concerns. When accepting agenda items make certain that they are ones that are acceptable to the group and not just one person's issues. If people bring up personal concerns that are not appropriate to the group, you may offer to talk with them privately and be prepared to make referrals if necessary. This is a remote possibility, but when dealing with this topic, individual concerns may emerge.

Model

Once the agenda has been set, you will want to give an overview of the fear cycle (Figure 1.1) and the primary prevention model (Figure 1.2) for identifying and treating fear and stress (see Section 1 of Part I: Overview of Fears and Stress). The strategies and developmental interventions will be addressed during a later session. At this point, you want them to develop a grasp of the development of fears and stress and help them to understand the fear and stress cycle. You may wish to make a slide of Figure 1.1 and Figure 1.2 to assist you in your brief overview of the model.

After presenting the model, you will need to discuss the sources and signs of stress. If the Fears and Stress Assessment Form (FSAF) on page 204 was completed in advance, you will want to ask the group to discuss in small groups of five or six members the responses they made on the survey. If you are introducing the FSAF during this session, allow time for the participants to complete it and then discuss in small groups.

You are referred to Sources of Fear in Children from the Introduction. You will want to share these data with the group and make comparisons with their responses. Do not share the responses in their small groups.

A brief overview of what will take place during the next session is appropriate here before adjourning.

Bibliography

Robinson, E. H., Rotter, J. C., Robinson, S., & Fey, M. (1992). Coping with fear and stress, *The School Counselor*.

Session 1
Outline

I. Opening Activity   20 minutes
    Explore environment, train station, or human bingo

II. Recollection of early childhood fears   15 minutes
    (see FSAF, page 204)
    Overview
    Agenda setting

III. Discuss model (include assessment instrument   25 minutes
    if not completed prior to workshop)
    Sources and signs of fear and stress
    (feedback on FSS is used)
    See Table 1.2 on page 26 (Normative Data on Children's Fears)

Fear and Stress Assessment Form (FSAF)

Identify a Situation
Or incident that is a source of fear or stress in your setting
> Example
> Student comes in upset about a friend's death

Affect
How you felt?
> Concerned, sad

Cognition
What you told yourself?
> I need to get this student to stop crying

Behavior
How did you respond to the client?
> Non-supportive, I did not validate student's feelings

Self-perception
Success or failure
> Failure

Insights
Related personal or past experiences
> Unresolved grief over my own mother's death

Current Impact
Still a stressor?
> Yes

Coping
Who or what helped?
> It helped to talk with a colleague and do this assessment

Session 2: Primary Prevention

The purpose of this session is to address the three levels of primary prevention as presented on pages 21-24. An overview of the levels will be discussed followed by an in-depth study of the first level of prevention and related intervention strategies.

Warm-up Activity

Ask the participants to sit comfortably, close their eyes if they choose, and imagine a small wooden or metal box or safe. The box is made of sturdy material with a hinged lid that can be secured by a padlock. Ask them to gather all of the bits and pieces of unfinished business and place them one by one in the box, e.g., a leaky faucet at home, questions like, Did I turn off the stove? Will I have enough gas in my car to get home?, Will I get my papers graded tonight? Take all of these loose ends and unrelated issues to today's session and place them securely in the box. Then ask them to secure the padlock to lock the box holding these items for safekeeping until they choose to remove them. Have them place the key in a safe place for retrieval later. Not that all these issues are safely stored, tell them they can focus entirely on today's topic without interferences. After they have completed this fantasy ask them to open their eyes and continue to maintain their comfortable position. This activity will help them to focus on the topic at hand by temporarily ridding them of all the potential external interferences. It also allows them to relax and focus on a collective activity. This activity can be modified for use with students to help them with concentration (Tubesing & Tubesing, 1986).

Levels of Prevention

Three levels of prevention are presented in the first part of this book. Level one focuses on the normative fears and stress of childhood such as fear of the dark, first day of school, or moving to a new city, state or country. The emphasis in level one is not on the fears but on preventive approaches to help children develop the concepts of control, security, and self-worth.

The activities from Sections 2 and 3 in Part I should be introduced during this session. Select one of the fear-specific from Section 2 and one of the fear-prevention activities from Section 3 to demonstrate with the group. Ask the teachers to again tap their imaginations and fantasize a classroom situation as they participate in the activities.

In the discussion that follows the fear-specific activity, point out the difference between episodic fears or situational stress and generalized fears or chronic stress. Episodic fears, such as moving to a new city or changing schools, can be addressed specifically while generalized fears, such as fear of strangers, are more difficult to observe. Each, however, can be anticipated and preventive approaches can be used to alleviate the potential chronic long-term problems that can be manifested. The long-term effects of fear and stress can, in fact, be debilitating emotionally and physically. Withdrawal from certain activities and development of physical ailments can result if appropriate skills and attitudes are not established early in life.

Level one approaches to the prevention of the debilitating effects of fear and stress are, therefore, significant to the way children will learn to deal with events throughout their lives. The focus here is on problem solving and decision-making, two critical skills for dealing with both episodic and generalized fear and stress. Children who develop effective problem solving and decision-making skills will recognize that they have control over their lives and, therefore, will experience a greater sense of security and self-worth both in school and elsewhere. According to Norman Sprinthall, the whole point of the concept of primary prevention is to create classroom educative experiences that affect student's intellectual and personal development simultaneously (Gerler & Anderson, 1986).

References

Gerler, E. R. & Anderson, R. F. (1986). The effects of classroom guidance on children's success in school. *Journal of Counseling and Development, 65,* 78-81.

Humphrey, J. H. (1998). *Helping children manage stress: A guide for adults.* Washington, DC: Child Welfare League of America.

Tubesing, N. L., & Tubesing, D. A. (1986). *Structural exercises in stress management.* Duluth, MN: Whole Person Press.

Tuebsing, N. L. & Christian, S. S. (1995). *Structured exercises in stress management.* Duluth, MN: Whole Person Associates.

Session 2
Outline

I. Activity   10 minutes

II. Levels of Prevention   20 minutes
    Primary Prevention   See Figure 1.2
    High Risk   Page 25
    Non-Coping   (Primary Prevention
                                   of Children's Fears)

III. Primary Prevention Activities   45 minutes
    Episodic fears and stress,   See Figure 1.1, page 22
    e.g., moving to new city;   (Fear Cycle)
    Generalizable fears and stress,
    e.g., fear of the dark

IV. Decision-making and Problem-solving Skills

Session 3: School and Classroom Activities

The purpose of this session is to help teachers and other school personnel develop ideas for activities that they can do with children to help them in developing the knowledge and skills necessary for coping with fear and stress. A further purpose is to help school personnel understand the way environment can contribute to fear and stress and develop strategies to help children cope.

Overview

The session should be opened with an activity from Section 2 or Section 3 in **Part 1: Overview of Fears and Stress in Children**. Pick an activity that you think participants will enjoy that can relate to a number of different curriculum areas. **Feeling Masks** for instance can relate to art, social studies, language arts, etc. The activity helps children to cope with fear and stress by learning to verbalize their worries. A number of research studies support the positive effects of cathartic release when dealing with stress or fear by just getting it off your chest.

Discuss how the activity can be used in the classroom not only to develop coping for fear or stress but also as a part of class content. Art: use of mixed media, understanding the use of colors, principles of drawing, etc. Social studies: how the way we feel affects how we relate to others. Language Arts: poetry reading and construction, speaking skills, etc.

After the activity, break the group into small groups by grade level or subject. Have the participants find three other activities in Section 2 or Section 3 of Part I that they could integrate into the curriculum. Have each group report to the whole group on the activities they discussed and share how they could use the activity as a part of the subject they are teaching.

Take a minute to talk about how many of the activities can be integrated into the curriculum. Also discuss the idea that they may want to do some activities just because they may help children develop ways of coping with fear and stress. Children who cannot concentrate on the learning task at hand because of their level of stress or fear are not actively engaged in learning. Helping them deal with their problems can increase the time on task for learning. Remember time on task is not the time the teacher spends teaching. Time on task is the time the child spends learning. Ten to twenty minutes per day spent building wellness in children can have tremendous benefits in cognitive learning. For example, there is supporting research to indicate that children who exercise, learn relaxation techniques, learn to communicate and make friends, develop confidence in self, and learn effective personal decision-making skills, and so on, are more inclined to do better on cognitive tasks.

Break into small groups and ask participants to brainstorm those things about school or community that are stressful for children. Discuss these in the whole group. The very structure of the school can be stressful. Most schools are competitive in nature, stressing individual goals and the concept of winners and losers.

To underline this idea, have everyone line up in a straight line. After they are all lined up say, OK, we're going to have a spelling bee. Ask the first person in line to spell cat, the next person dog, the next jump, etc. Ask the fourth or fifth person to spell lactobacillus. Before the person becomes embarrassed, call off the spelling bee. The spelling bee is the perfect example of an individual competitive environment. Some children thrive in this type of environment while others give up in order to avoid the stress and fear of failure, embarrassment, etc. Others turn the stress inward. Too much competition creates a lot of losers and few winners. While there may always be a place for competition, the research is very strong that cooperative learning can decrease stress and increase learning outcomes. Show how the spelling bee could become cooperative or competitive in two or more groups competing with each other but on a cooperative team, i.e., divide class into three groups, each person must spell a word, but that person may consult with two members of their group before spelling the word. Let them make an imaginary phone call to an expert. You can be a consultant once every 2, 3, or 4 times. A number of reactions are possible. Now show how spelling can be a completely cooperative venture. Last week we had ten spelling words, and we have ten people in the class. Ten words were spelled correctly for the whole class. This week we will work for 75 words correct. I have divided the class into study groups. Your task is to help everyone learn the words for Friday. If intrinsic motivation is not enough say, then say when we get 75, we will (include appropriate extrinsic motivator). If not, we will try again next week.

Human Spring: To underline the concept, ask people if they have ever done leg wrestling or arm wrestling where two people compete and at the end there is a winner who feels good and a loser who does not. Have the participants pair up for human spring. Ask each pair to stand 2-3 feet apart, pull up their hands, palms out toward their partner. Each person leans into his or her partner so that both are off balance but sustained by each other like a pyramid or triangle. Then ask them to push each other back to a standing position, increase the distance each other and try again. The goal is to see how far apart two people can get and still help each other return to a standing position without anyone losing their balance. No one loses and each pair is working to accomplish a goal together.

Take a few minutes to brainstorm how the classroom and or school could do more cooperative learning and play activities to decrease stress.

What other environmental stressors did you discuss earlier: What else can the group come up with to deal with these? (You may wish to carry this discussion over to Session 4.)

Materials

Materials needed for this group activity include enough material to make one Feeling Mask per participant. For time restraints, you may wish to make masks out of paper plates or paper bags in which case you need plates, bags, scissors, crayons or markers, glue, and tongue depressors for the paper plates.

References

Allen, J. S., Klein, R. J., & Holden, M. (eds.) (1997). *Ready, set, relax: A research-based program of relaxation, learning and self-esteem for children*. Inner Coaching.

Johnson, D., & Johnson, R. (1987). *Learning together and alone*. Englewood Cliffs, NJ:Prentice Hall.

Johnson, D., Johnson, R., & Holubec, E. (1991). *Cooperation in the classroom*. Edina, MN: Interaction Book Company.

Johnson, D., Johnson, R., & Holubec, E. (1990). *Circles of learning*. Englewood Cliffs, NJ: Prentice Hall.

Johnson, D., Johnson, R., & Holubec, E. (1994). *New circles of learning: Cooperation in the classroom and school.* Alexandria, VA: Association for Supervision and Curriculum Development.

Weinstein, M., & Goodman, J. (1981). *Playfare.* Atascadero, CA: Impact Press.

Williams, M. L. & Burke, D. O. (1996). Cool cats, calm kids: Relaxation and stress *management for young people.* Atascadero, CA: Impact Publishers.

Session 3
Outline

I. Activity from Part I: Discussion and Activities   30 minutes
(Feeling Masks, etc.)

II. Discussion on how activities can be used for   10 minutes
Fear and stress as well as in subject areas.
Pick out several other activities from Part I
And discuss how they can be used.

III. Small group brainstorming on Environmental   10 minutes
Stressors

IV. Spelling Bee   10 minutes

V. Discussion — Competition vs. Cooperation   15 minutes

VI. Human Spring   5 minutes

VII. Discussion   10 minutes
Other environmental stressors and how might
you deal with them?

Session 4: Helping High Risk Children

The purpose of this session is to help teachers and other school personnel recognize potential high-risk children and to develop the knowledge and skills necessary for helping these children.

Overview

High-risk children are those who are more susceptible to fear and stress and more likely to suffer possible ill effects of fear or stress. Children who move to a new area for the first time, children whose language is not the language of instruction, children whose parents are separated or divorced, children who have experienced traumatic events or disasters, children whose values or culture place a great deal of emphasis on specific behaviors or goals such as academic success as measured by grades or test scores, and children with learning difficulties are examples of high-risk children.

Start off the session with an activity that highlights one of these groups, e.g., children for which the language of instruction is not their native language. An activity that can be used is to ask half the group to leave the room for a minute and wait just outside. Give the remaining participants instructions to tell the person they are paired with when the others return to do a simple task (e.g., write your name on the board, put that piece of paper in the trash can, give me your book, spell the word cat). These tasks must be spoken in a foreign language. If the individual knows a language that their partner does not know they may use that language, otherwise be creative and make up a word "Dr. Seuss style" for each word in the instructions. For example, "put that piece of paper in the trash can," could be written, "Urn dar cue vo yerd we na dina tur." You may wish to have several of these already made up on slips of paper. Tell the people who will assign the task to be forceful and act as if the person should know what you are saying. If they don't respond, say it louder and be even more demanding. Give people a minute to memorize the new language then ask the others to rejoin the group. Have the participants pair off, one to assign the task paired with one who has been out of the room. Explain to the outsiders that they will be asked to perform a simple classroom task that any third grader can do, and they will repeat the task until it is done or until time is called.

Give the participants a few minutes, repeating the command five or six times. Some will probably give hints through body language. Stop the activity and let people settle back in their seats to discuss the activity. How did you feel knowing it was a simple task but not knowing what was said? How did you look for hints on what to do? Have you ever been anywhere where you did not know the language and you were trying to figure out what to do? How was your stress level in such a situation? Why is it a stressful situation? Discuss your own frustrations with language barriers, if any, in your school.

Define "At-Risk Children" with the group and brainstorm groups of children at your school that may fall into this category.

Break into groups and discuss ways to help the at-risk child, e.g., a student who is facing a new place, new school, and new people. Just because someone has done it before doesn't mean it's not stressful. Uprooting someone's routine is often hard on adults, but it can be just as hard on children. Little things we don't think about can be stressful. For example, "How do I get my lunch?" "Where do I put my books?" can be very stressful to a child. To help children assimilate to a new setting you can assign a friendly helper student to show them the routine. You can ask that new students not be brought to the classroom and dropped off in the middle of the day. Instead, ask parents to please bring their child back first thing in the morning because you would like time to make arrangements for the child's first day. This gives the teacher time to prepare and plan to make the new student feel welcome to the class.

Give groups time to discuss strategies they might use. Use Appendix I-A, page 113, and Appendix II-A, page 185, as a vehicle for discussion.

Bring the groups back together and ask them to share their discussions with the whole group.

Introduce the concept of the single child at risk. This is a child that doesn't fit any categories the school defines as "at risk" but is, nonetheless, a child under a lot of stress. What are the signs of stress for a child? How can you tell that a child is under stress? You may wish to brainstorm this question before you pass out the list of signs of stress in children (see Section 1 of Part I).

Materials

Strips of paper with directions for simple classroom tasks written in English and in a foreign or made up language. Chalkboard or chart and holder with chart paper for recording brainstorming ideas.

References

Adams, J. D. (1980). *Understanding and managing stress: A facilitator's guide.* San Diego, CA: University Associates.

Haggerty, R. J., Sherrod, L. R., Garmezy, N., & Rutter, M. J. (1996). *Stress, risk, and resilience in children and adolescents: Processes, mechanisms, and interventions.*Cambridge, UK: Cambridge University Press.

Henderson, N. & Milstein, M. (1996). *Resiliency in schools: Making it happen for students and educators.* Thousand Oaks, CA: Corwin Press.

Miller, S. M. (1982). *Child stress: Understanding and answering stress signals of infants, children, and teenagers.* Garden City, NY: Doubleday.

Schultz, E., & Hurshurt, C. (1983). *Childhood stress and the school experience.* New York: Human Science Press.

Stroebel, E., & Stroebel, C. (1980). *Kiddie QR: A choice for children.* Wethersfield, CT: QR Institute.

Witkin, G. (1999). Kidstress: *What it is, how it feels, how to help.* New York: Viking.

Session 4
Outline

I. Activity   20 minutes
   (Simple classroom task in foreign languages)

II. Discuss activity   10 minutes

III. Define "At Risk Children" and present example;   10 minutes
    brainstorm group of at-risk children

IV. Present example of how you might help one   20 minutes
    at-risk group (new student);
    break into groups and brainstorm strategies for
    other at-risk groups

V. Small group sharing strategies   10 minutes

VI. Discuss concept of the single child at   20 minutes
    risk and the signs of stress

Session 5: Helping Children During a Crisis

The purpose of this session is to help participants develop an understanding of how to help children cope with their fears and stress during a crisis. A crisis might include a collective crisis such as the assassination of a political leader or natural disaster such as an earthquake or an individual crisis like the loss of a parent.

Overview

Open the session with an activity. One suggestion is to give each participant a piece of modeling clay. Tell them they may mold it as they see fit while you talk. Ask people to close their eyes and remember a time of crisis and what they were doing at the time. For example, where were you when the terrorist attacks occurred on September 11th? Although this was a collectively shared event, each person reacts a bit differently but most have strong emotional memories.

Another activity is to ask them to read an anthology or a poem depicting a tragic event and ask them to pay attention to the emotions emitted while reading the piece. A third possibility is to show a clip from a movie depicting an emotion-laden event.

Notice what people do with the clay as you go through the recollection or reflection process. Ask participants if they were aware of what they did with the clay (some will probably just hold it, some will just kneed it, and some may make shapes and forms).

Discussion: One teacher used clay at story time to help children deal with the stress of a crisis around them. Teachers would pass out clay, give children a chance to talk about what was going on around them, and then read a story. As the days went by, children would knead less and begin making things with the clay. Clay and play can be a great tension release for children.

During and after a crisis or traumatic event, it is important to keep to a routine but not ignore the events or the feelings people have about the events surrounding them. It is important that you let children have the opportunity to discuss or express their feelings about the crisis. It is also important not to dwell on events. Answer factual questions with accurate factual responses. A crisis often reminds children what little control they have over their lives and leaves them feeling vulnerable. Emphasize the control they do have. "It seems you handled that well. I see you are sorting this mess out."

Hand out Appendix II-A, II-B, II-C, II-D, and II-E to the group. Break into small groups. Have each grade level or appropriate group (primary, intermediate, etc.) meet together and discuss the handouts. How would they give emotional first aid to children this age? Verbal catharsis can be difficult for preschool or kindergarten children. Expressing their feelings through art or play might be better.

Give the small groups an additional task of determining what to do after the crisis to help children. Although the emotions of a crisis will be dissipating, the "after crisis" emotions can still be strong. Look through Part I:

Overview of Fears and Stress in Children and discuss activities that would be helpful to your age group in dealing with the aftermath of a traumatic event.

In the groups have participants share how they help children deal with personal crises such as the loss of a parent. Read *The Fall of Freddie, The Leaf* or another book that talks about death and discuss how books can be used with children to help them cope.

End the session with a relaxation activity. You can use the scripts from Part I or develop your own. You can use guided imagery or physical relaxation or a combination of these. This could be helpful in a crisis and/or as a preventive technique that can help children on a day-to-day basis.

Materials

Script for opening exercise and clay. Video and equipment or anthology/poetry if used to depict emotional event. Script for relaxation activity. Book or chart for recording if desired. Handouts from Appendix II-A through II-E.

References

Crabbs, M. A. (1981). School mental health services following an environmental disaster. *Journal of School Health, 51,* 165-167.

Gordon, N. S., Farberow, N., & Maida, C. A. (1999). *Manual for children and disasters (series in trauma and loss).* Levittown, PA: Brunner/Mazel.

Monahon, C. (1997). *Children and trauma: A guide for parents and professionals.* San Francisco, CA: Josey-Bass.

Rotter, J. C., & Robinson, E. H. (1987). Coping with fear and stress: Classroom intervention. *International Quarterly, 5*(4), 39-45.

Schwarz, J. H. (1982). Guiding children's creative expression in the stress of war. *Stress and Anxiety, 8,* 351-354.

Session 5
Outline

I.	Activity: Remember When	10 minutes
II.	Mini Lecture/Discussion Tips on Helping Children in a Crisis	15 minutes
III.	Small Group Activity Handouts: Emotional First Aid Developmental Differences	20 minutes
IV.	Small Group Activity After the First Aid	10 minutes
V.	Activity: Read book on loss; give examples of discussion questions that might be used	10 minutes
VI.	Discussion: How do teachers help children in personal crisis?	10 minutes
VII.	Relaxation and/or guided imagery activity	10 minutes

Session 6: Helping Children Who Are Not Coping Well

The purpose of this session is to help teachers and other school personnel develop an understanding of how to help children who are not coping well in their life because of the effects of fear and stress; to help participants identify potential resources for helping children; and to provide strategies for those who wish to help children work through their difficulties.

Overview

Begin the session by reviewing the prevention model discussed earlier in Session 1. The last stage of prevention is helping those children who are experiencing the effects of fear or stress in negative, self-defeating ways. The longer debilitating fears or stress go untreated, the harder they are to treat and the more likely they are to become worse and more disruptive in the child's life. Helping a child when fear initially becomes disruptive can prevent adversity and a deepening of the current problem.

Discuss the information presented in Section 1 of Part I: Overview of Fears and Stress in Children. You may wish to ask participants to read this before the session. In the discussion, highlight the stages of helping a child with a fear-related problem. Point out the need for the child to be able to talk honestly and openly to someone they trust; someone that will not make fun of them or belittle their fears. Good general communication skills are needed here.

Also point out the importance of assessment. Is this a child with a fear or a fearful child? Although both need help, and many of the same activities or techniques may help both, the goal is slightly different. The teacher may help the fearful child deal with one fear to find it quickly replaced with another. Here the emphasis should be on helping the child develop a sense of worth, control, and security. On the other hand, a child may generally cope well but develop a fear of a specific object. Here help should be directed at coping with that specific fear.

Next, as a group, brainstorm the mental health resources of your community. Where can children get help with stress, fears, and phobias? How can children in need be referred to these resources? What are the costs of these resources? Here the facilitator will want to do some homework on these questions before the group meets. Are there local counselors, psychologists, psychiatric social workers or nurses, or psychiatrists who are available to serve children with fear-related and stress-related problems? Is there anyone else on the school staff trained and willing to help?

Next the facilitator may wish to conduct an activity for the teachers to help them come to terms with the role they can play in helping children struggling with fears and stress. In some schools and communities, there will be no help available. The teacher is truly the only "mental health" resource. In other cases, the teacher will have additional resources. It is important for teachers to decide how much help they feel they can provide; what kinds of problems they feel trained to help with. You may wish to put these and other questions on a sheet of paper for each participant. Have participants fill them out individually then get together and have a discussion. Everyone can share the highlights of their group's discussion with the larger group. You may find a couple of teachers on each level who have had some counseling experience and who are willing to work with children or team up with teachers to help them work with children.

Present a mini-lecture on the topic. If you are going to help, what do you do? Many of the fear-prevention activities for high-risk children in the classroom may be adapted to be appropriate for individual work. You may wish to suggest how several of these activities could be applied. One of the most common techniques for helping children deal with extreme fear is systematic desensitization. A discussion of this treatment is contained in Part I. Present this concept and demonstrate the procedure.

Discuss with the group when this might be a good approach with a child. Have the group pair off and role play or use a real fear if volunteered by one of the pairs such as fear of bridges, snakes, or elevators.

Materials

Information from Section 1 in Part I: Overview of Fears and Stress in Children. Clarification sheet on questions teachers should ask.

References

Arnold, L. E. (Ed.) (1990). *Childhood stress.* New York: John Wiley and Sons.

Eisen, A. R. & Kearney, C. A. (1995). *Practitioner's guide to treating fear and anxiety in children and adolescents: A cognitive-behavioral approach.* Northvale, NJ: Jason Aronson, Inc.

Morris, R. J., & Kratochwill, T. R. (1983). *Treating children's fears and phobias.* New York: Pergamon Press.

Wolman, B. B. (1978). *Children's fears.* New York: Grosset and Dunlop.

Session 6
Outline

I. Mini Lecture and Discussion: 10 minutes
Review of primary prevention, counseling
model, stages of helping, fearful child or child
with a fear.

II. Brainstorm and Discussion: Mental Health   5 minutes
Resources in School and Community

III. Teacher's Role and Feelings of Competence   20 minutes

IV. Mini Lecture on Techniques of Helping   15 minutes
Individual Child With Fear and Stress

V. Presentation and Demonstration of   15 minutes
Systematic Desensitization

VI. Practice Systematic Desensitization   25 minutes

Session 7: Stress/Fear and the Family

The purpose of this session is to emphasize that fear and stress are family issues. Although isolated incidences may trigger fear and stress, their effect on children often results from the amount of advance preparation that family members have made and their ability to effectively follow up on stressful situations.

Overview

This session is optional and may be incorporated in one of the other sessions. It is important, however, that family-related issues be addressed at some time during the training. You may want to start a discussion with the teachers, then ask them to identify specific incidences they have encountered with crises or with which they are familiar. Ask them to share, in small groups, how an incident was handled and the affect it had on the children and their families.

It is often difficult to determine, during times of crises, how much to share with children. This will vary depending on the age and developmental level of the child. However, it is important to keep the lines of communication open. Ignoring or minimizing an incident can cause more harm than a forthright discussion of the issues. Children who have established a sense of control, security, and self-worth are more likely to deal with the situation knowing that they have a support system within the family and the community. When information is withheld or questions ignored, that support system can become eroded.

The debilitating effects of stress and fear can be reduced, if not prevented, by taking care of oneself and maintaining the family as a unit. Through proper nutritional habits, regular exercise, some form of relaxation, and open communication, families can learn that taking care of themselves can serve as a very useful tool during a time of crisis. Having a plan and maintaining open lines of communication can foster these necessary qualities of control, security, and self-worth so essential during times of stress.

In order to personalize the issues related to families and stress and fear, ask the participants to take a moment to reflect upon their own family of origin. Ask them to recall the themes and values expressed within their families and to write down a family motto that was prevalent when they were growing up. Examples might include: "The family that plays together stays together." "Honesty is the best policy." When they have identified their family motto ask them to share it with the group. Next, begin a discussion of whether these mottos hold true for them and their families today. These mottos represent some very basic values that can have an impact on the way they conduct themselves in times of crisis.

Discuss the attachments located at the end of this session regarding family stress. Finally, ask them to complete the Family Stressor Intervention Plan.

References

Arent, R. P. (1984). *Stress and your child: A parents guide to symptoms and strategies.* Englewood Cliffs, NJ: Prentice Hall.

Arent, R. P. (1992). Trust building with children who hurt: A one-to-one support *program for children ages 5-14.* West Nyack, NY: Center for Applied Research in Education.

Curran, D. (1985). *Stress and the healthy family.* Minneapolis: Winston Press.

Dacey, J. S., Fiore, L. B., & Ladd, G. T. (2000). *Your anxious child: How parents and teachers can relieve anxiety in children.* San Francisco, CA: Josey-Bass.

Elkind, D. (1989). *The hurried child: Growing up too fast too soon.* Reading, MA: Addison-Wesley.

Faber, A., Mazlish, E. (1999). *How to talk so kids will listen and listen so kids will talk.* New York: Avon Books.

Miller, S. M. (1982). *Childstress! Understanding and answering stress signals of infants,children and teenagers.* Garden City, NY: Doubleday.

United States Department of State. (1986). *Managing children during a crisis.* Washington, DC: Author.

Session 7
Outline

I.	Overview of Family Stress	15 minutes
II.	Small Group Discussion of Incidents	20 minutes
III.	Discuss Healthy Prevention Activities Proper Nutrition, Exercise, Relaxation	10 minutes
IV.	Family Motto Activity	10 minutes
V.	Discuss Family Stressors and Ways to Mediate Family Stress	15 minutes
VI.	Family Stressor Intervention Plan	20 minutes

Top Ten Family Stresses

1) Economics/finances/budgeting

2) Children's behavior/discipline/sibling fighting

3) Insufficient couple time

4) Lack of shared responsibility in the family

5) Communicating with children

6) Insufficient "me" time

7) Guilt for not accomplishing more

8) Spousal relationship (communication, friendship, sex)

9) Insufficient family playtime

10) Overscheduled family calendar

Source: Curran, D. (1985). *Stress and the healthy family.* Minneapolis: Winston Press.

Ways to Mediate Family Stress

1) Establish family traditions

2) Discuss family values

3) Take on something bigger than yourself

4) Respect differences within the family

5) Exercise together

6) Emphasize wellness instead of illness

7) Allow for private time

8) Become active in a community organization that includes children and adults

9) Take on a family project

10) Learn success imagery

11) Turn problems into challenges

12) Hold family meetings

13) Develop and utilize effective communication skills

14) Show that you care about and respect the other family members

15) Go to entertainment together

16) Provide a job within the family for every member

17) Listen

18) Emphasize cooperative dietary planning— adults setting good examples

19) Eat one meal a day as a family to discuss day's events

20) Laugh together

Source: Rotter, M. F. (1985). *Stress is a family affair.* Presentation at AACD Convention, Los Angeles.

Self-Management Techniques

Good Nutritional Habits
1. Balanced diet
   a. Sufficient vitamins, minerals, protein, complex carbohydrates and fiber
   b. Minimized consumption of sugar, salt, saturated fats, refined white flour and chemical additives

2. Regular meals

3. Maintenance of recommended weight

4. Moderate use of alcohol and caffeine

5. No smoking

Good Exercise Habits
1. Regular aerobic exercise to improve cardiovascular fitness

2. Regular recreational exercise for tension reduction and diversion

Self-Awareness
1. Understanding of personal needs, preferences and idiosyncrasies

2. Assertive behavior and role negotiation

Letting Go Techniques
1. Regular relaxation habits (e.g., meditation, prayer, healing, visualization)

2. Seeking closure of tasks and interpersonal situations ...finishing unfinished business

Personal Planning
1. Effective time management day-to-day

2. Life and career planning for the long term

Source: Adams, J. D. (1980).*Understanding and managing stress: A book of readings.*San Diego: University Associates.

Family Stressor Intervention Plan

Family stressors:

Target stressor:

Identify desired outcome:

Determine strategy:

Apply strategy:

Determine level of success:

What will be your next step?

Who will be involved?

What will each person's (including yourself) role be?

What outside support systems are needed?

My personal time line — I will do the following:
Today

Tomorrow

Next Week

Session 8: Developing an Action Plan

The purpose of this session is to help teachers develop a plan of action to implement the activities on fear and stress in their schools. The emphasis will be on the three levels of prevention with a focus on integration of the activities into the daily curriculum.

Overview

This final session will address perhaps the most important part of the training, for it is through the plan of action developed by the participants that the program will or will not reach success. If the activities are not formally introduced into the curriculum, they lose potential impact. You want to challenge the participants to expand their skills in observing children and incorporate these methods of addressing some very basic human motivators. Without a sense of security, control, and self-worth one cannot become a fully-functioning human being. By addressing the predictable fears and stress of children, teachers can help them to accomplish these three basic ingredients for success in life.

An activity to help the participants to stretch their imaginations and expand their own sense of accomplishment follows. It is called "You are More Than You Think" and is adapted from an activity in Jean Houston's book, *The Possible Human* (1981).

Procedures for "You are More Than You Think":

1. Stand up and face the front of the room allowing arms length distance between yourself and others.
2. Extend right arm in front and turn head to the right and locate a point on the wall that is as far as you can see. Do not strain your neck muscles. Then turn head back to center and lower arm.
3. Extend left arm in front and turn head to the left. Then turn head back to center and lower arm.
4. Extend both arms from the side and with head remaining forward swing upper body and arms to the right and then to the left. Return to center and lower arms.
5. Extend right arm in front and turn head to the right picking a new point on the wall and notice how much further this point is than the first point. Do not strain your neck muscles.

Plan of Action

Congratulations for completing this training workshop on children's fear and stress. You should be better equipped to recognize the signs and sources of stress and fear in children and likewise introduce appropriate intervention strategies in your classroom, school, and community. If you have found these sessions to be effective and the materials appropriate for your setting, it will now be important for you to establish a plan of action.

Please complete the incomplete statements that follow and then share your responses with another member of the group:

I teach grade(s)_____

The level of fear or stress in my classroom, school, and/or community is:

The predominant fears and stress in my setting are:

I will begin to introduce the following strategies in my school or classroom during the year:

Level 1 Prevention

Level 2 Prevention

Level 3 Prevention

I have the following resources in my community to serve the children with problems related to fear and stress:

Closing Activities

Ask participants to work in groups of three to design a poster or bumper sticker (or other creative promotional product) related to the topic of the workshop. Example: FEAR IS A FOUR-LETTER WORD

Have participants complete a clustering around the words fear or stress. This can be done individually or as a group. Place and circle the word fear on the chalkboard or large newsprint so all can see, then ask individuals to free associate around the word, calling on different people in the group to call out one word at a time. Example: **F**antasy, **E**uphoria, **A**cceptance, **R**eal or such things as ghosts, afraid, fear dark, or night.

Continue to call on individuals until your board or newsprint is filled with circled and linked words. Then ask each person to construct a paragraph using as many of the words as possible. Ask volunteers to read their paragraphs. This activity again helps them to see the complexity of the issues related to fear and stress and also, since it comes at the end of the workshop, helps them to tie together much of what has been covered. It also enhances collegiality within the group by establishing a common interest. Finally, the activity can help to solidify a commitment to follow through with the plan of action.

References

Houston, J. (1981). *The possible human.* Boston: Houghton Mifflin.

Session 8
Outline